WHAT
WOULD
JESUS
READ?

WHAT WOULD JESUS READ?

DAILY DEVOTIONS THAT GUIDED THE SAVIOR

JOE AMARAL

Faith Words

NEW YORK   BOSTON   NASHVILLE

Unless otherwise noted, all Scripture references are taken from THE HOLY BIBLE, NEW INTERNATIONAL VERSION®, NIV® copyright © 1973, 1978, 1984, 2011 by Biblica, Inc.™ Used by permission. All rights reserved worldwide.

Scripture noted with NLT Holy Bible, New Living Translation copyright © 1996, 2004, 2007 by Tyndale House Foundation. Used by permission of Tyndale House Publishers Inc., Carol Stream, Illinois 60188. All rights reserved.

FaithWords
Hachette Book Group
237 Park Avenue
New York, NY 10017
www.faithwords.com

Printed in the United States of America
RRD-C

First Edition: August 2012
10 9 8 7 6 5 4 3 2 1

FaithWords is a division of Hachette Book Group, Inc.
The FaithWords name and logo are trademarks of Hachette Book Group, Inc.

The Hachette Speakers Bureau provides a wide range of authors for speaking events. To find out more, go to www.hachettespeakersbureau.com or call (866) 376-6591.

The publisher is not responsible for websites (or their content) that are not owned by the publisher.

Library of Congress Cataloging-in-Publication Data
Amaral, Joe.
What would Jesus read? : daily devotions that guided the Savior / Joe Amaral.—First edition
pages cm
ISBN 978-1-4555-0814-3
1. Devotional literature.   I. Title.
BS391.3.A63 2012
242'.2—dc23
2011047864

This book is dedicated to the Jewish people.
Thank you for your relentless tenacity in
preserving the Torah. We Christians
owe you a great debt of gratitude.

Contents

Contents

Preface

The Sabbath was the holy day of the Jews; the Temple was the holy place of the Jews; the Torah was the holy Scripture of the Jews...and as a Jew, of Jesus also.

After the destruction of the First Temple in Jerusalem, the Jews were exiled to Babylon. Not only was there no longer a physical place to go pray, even the sacred Scriptures were becoming scarce. Many of the biblical scrolls were lost or destroyed during the exile.

In an attempt to preserve the Scriptures, the rabbis divided up the biblical texts into weekly reading portions and distributed them among the families of Israel. Each family became responsible for memorizing their assigned passage and then reading it in the synagogue every Sabbath.

This system of reading is the basis for the story as found in Luke 4:16–17, "He went to Nazareth, where he had been brought up, and on the Sabbath day he went into the synagogue, as was his custom. And he stood up to read. The scroll of the prophet Isaiah was handed to him."

This system is still in use today by Jews all over the world. Now, for the first time, in *What Would Jesus Read?*, modern-day Christians have the opportunity to follow and practice the same devotional system Jesus used!

The weekly readings (parashah in Hebrew—parashoth

being the plural of parashah—meaning "portion" or "segment") are composed of two texts: one from the Torah and one from the Prophets. The reading cycle consists of 54 weekly readings for an annual total of 378 daily readings.

This devotional is purposely conversational in its style. Just imagine that we are sitting at a table with a small group and we are simply talking about the texts together. I've injected my personality and humor into the daily reading. For better or for worse, you're getting the real Joe!

For thirteen months I poured myself into this book. It has been a labor of love, and I hope that as you read you will find a new appreciation for God's Word.

WHAT
WOULD
JESUS
READ?

Genesis 1:3

Let there be light

Genesis is one of the most well-known books in the Bible. The biblical account of creation is known throughout the world. In these opening verses of the Bible we see the creative power of God at work. The world was void, the world was dark and it was without form. But then God spoke. He said let there be light, and there was light.

I could fill pages and pages describing how amazing the story of creation is, but instead I would like to focus on how these verses can relate to your life. Life isn't always fair. We have sunny days and we have dark days. Some people are living in constant spiritual and emotional darkness. They see no way out on their own. God speaks four simple words, *let there be light*. We can spend years looking for and seeking after natural solutions, but sometimes the greatest solution is right in front of our eyes.

Think about this: if the God of our universe could speak into actual darkness, then how much more is He able to speak into the darkness of our lives and bring us His light?

Genesis 3:13

What is this you have done?

Talk about definitive moments in history. Recorded in today's reading is the day sin entered into the world and changed the course of humanity for eternity.

God had created a perfect environment for Adam and Eve to live in: Fruit-bearing trees. No sickness or disease. No evil. What a paradise! They were allowed to enjoy everything in the garden; everything except for one tree, that is.

Isn't that like human nature? You put a child in a room and tell him that he can play with any toy he wants, but he can't touch anything in a specific drawer. So where is the first place he goes when you leave the room? You guessed it…the forbidden drawer.

Adam blames Eve; Eve blames the snake. No one wants to take responsibility. There's plenty of blame to go around! Our human nature always wants to push the boundaries. All we have to do is live within God's guidelines. Don't fight God's laws—obey them and understand that He has placed them there for your protection and blessing.

Genesis 4:7

Sin is crouching at your door

Sibling rivalry is nothing new, but at the heart of this story is jealousy. God accepted Abel's offering, but not Cain's. He must have been moping around because God basically said to him, "Why the long face?" God sees into his heart and even warns him. He's basically telling Cain to guard his heart and let go of the bitterness. Then comes the statement: "Sin is crouching at your door."

Didn't Cain realize that there would be hundreds, if not thousands, of opportunities to present offerings to the Lord? But Cain just couldn't let it go. So in his sin he rises up and kills his brother.

Okay, so maybe you're not planning to kill a sibling, but maybe there is some jealousy in your life. And if you don't deal with it, it will continue to rise until perhaps it causes you to sin.

Receive God's warning today. Deal with the anger or resentment in your heart before it causes you to do something you will regret for eternity.

Genesis 5:1

In the likeness of God

There are a lot of difficult concepts to grasp in this world. Some people devote their entire lives to studying the origins of the universe. Others devote themselves to finding cures for humanity's many diseases. The concept in today's reading is the most staggering one of them all.

The God of our universe could have formed man after anything He wanted to. And yet He chose to form man in His own image. If you stop and think about it, it's an incredible thought. What that says to me is that I'm important. It means you're important.

Many people struggle with their self-image. Some people spend a fortune trying to improve who they are and how they look. Keep this thought in your heart today: you are created in the image and likeness of God. You can't put a price tag on something like that. Just accept this fact: you're great just the way you are.

Don't let the world tell you how you should look or how you should act. If you focus and devote your life to being more like Him . . . you'll be just fine.

Genesis 6:5

Evil all the time

God created the earth out of love. He desires to have fellowship with the very creation that He has made. He wants to walk with us and talk with us, He wants to know us. He wants us to live in paradise and to live a sin-free life.

Because of the sin of Adam and Eve our hearts now are naturally inclined to sin. The sin became so great that God decided it was time for a clean slate. Could it be true that, as the text says, all man thought about was sin? Some might say that's an exaggeration. But let's be honest with ourselves, let's examine our own hearts. It's not a place we like to go, but the truth is, evil does live there. Look at the world around us; watch the news. The evidence is overwhelming: man's heart is evil.

No one is above sin... no one! We have all incurred Adam's sin. It's in our nature now. The key is to find out how to keep it under control.

So how do we fix it? We don't. Only God can. Give God an all-access pass to your heart. Let His Law and love fill your heart like a flood.

Genesis 6:8

Noah found favor

How many nice people would you say you know? Define what makes a person nice. Let's take it a step further. How many people do you know that you would consider to be righteous? I don't know about you, but I have a pretty short list. I know a lot of people who think they're righteous. But that's an entirely different devotional. We all think that we're okay, but how do we really measure up to God's standards?

Consider Noah. We don't know much about him. We do know about the world in which he lived. From the text we learn that the people around him were living for themselves...that they weren't living for God. We learn that everybody was living as they pleased. But right in the middle of this text comes this remarkable statement: Noah found favor in the eyes of God.

I don't know about you, but I want that to be said of me. I want to live my life in a way that is pleasing to God. If we read His word and if we listen to His voice, then we also can find favor in the eyes of God.

Isaiah 43:2

When you pass through the waters,
I will be with you

As you read through the Torah, one thing becomes perfectly clear—the nation of Israel was not perfect. Over and over again God provides for them, protects them, and does incredible things in their presence, yet they sin and turn away from Him. On more than one occasion God was planning to either punish or destroy them. But every time they repented, God relented. He forgave their sin and kept His promises.

This passage beautifully describes God's heart toward the nation of Israel. He uses such tender and loving language. He assures them that they will never be alone, that He will always walk with them.

This passage isn't only for Israel, it applies to us today. You can have the confidence that God is with you, that He will be with you through the good and the bad. Even when we fall, all we have to do is turn back to Him and He will be there waiting for us. So if you're passing through some turbulent waters, be at peace and know that God will never leave you and that He will always watch over you.

Genesis 6:9

*Noah was a righteous man, blameless among
the people of his time*

When God asked Noah to build the ark, it had never rained before. No one had ever seen rain, so when God asked Noah to build this massive boat, what must Noah have thought? I wonder if he questioned the command. Perhaps he tried to reason his way out of it. Surely God wasn't asking him to do this; maybe Noah thought this was his own bright idea.

Have you ever wondered how large the ark actually was? I knew it was big, but I never realized how big until I saw the world's only full-size replica in Hong Kong. This ark was huge! No wonder it took so long to build. Being able to walk through the ark in Hong Kong gave me a whole new appreciation for Noah's commitment and obedience to God's command.

Have you ever had a dream or a vision so big that you questioned God as the source of it? Instead of giving in to the pressure or bowing to the ridicule of the people, Noah stuck to the calling the Lord gave him. In the end, it not only saved his life, but also the lives of all those he loved.

Genesis 8:21

*The L*ORD *smelled the pleasing aroma and*
said in His heart

What would you consider to be a pleasing aroma? Maybe a freshly brewed cup of coffee in the morning? That would be my first choice, but to God, sacrifice was the aroma that got His attention. During the days of the flood, there was only one way to make atonement for your sins: blood. There was no quick prayer to be said or any simple solution. The only way to remove the stain of sin was the shedding of blood. (We're talking before the days of the Temple or Tabernacle.) There was no orderly way to do this. A clean animal had to die on your behalf. This would become the foundation for the temple practices.

What is striking here is that to God, the sacrifice was a pleasing aroma to His nostrils. When an animal is brought to an altar and has its blood shed, God calls that pleasing.

Have you ever responded to an altar call in church? Remember this: things go to the altar to die. What thought, attitude, or emotion in your life needs to die? And when it does, it is pleasing to God.

Genesis 9:9

*I now establish my covenant with you and with
your descendants after you*

What does the word "covenant" mean to you? It's not
a term that we use in our modern-day vocabulary. As a
result, the power of its meaning has been lost or diluted.
Most people would define it as a promise that one person
makes to another. One definition states that a covenant is
a binding contract.

In other words, it's not something that you would take
lightly. We live in a world where promises are both made
and broken on a daily basis. But what about God? Does He
make promises He cannot or does not keep? Of course not.

God established the covenant with us because He knew
that we as human beings would never be able to hold up
our end of the bargain.

With Noah He covenanted never to flood the earth
again. Has God made a covenant with you? He said that
He would always be with us, that He will never abandon
us. He always keeps His promises. The Scriptures encourage us to be imitators of God . . . let's be people of our word.

Genesis 11:4

*Come, let us build ourselves a city, with a tower
that reaches to the heavens*

The infamous Tower of Babel. What did the people do that was so bad? They wanted to build a tall tower. Is that such a sin? Don't we build tall buildings all the time today? So what was it about this particular tower that caused God to react the way He did?

You see, it wasn't *what* they wanted to build, but *why* they wanted to build. The text says that they wanted to make a name for themselves. They wanted to lift themselves up above the very Creator. If there is anything we learn from the Torah, it's this: God is a jealous God. He never wants to hold second place in your life.

If we only live to lift up ourselves and to make a name for ourselves, then we are going to have a very shallow existence. Life is temporary; we need to set our sights on those things that are eternal. Take the focus off yourself; start living to serve and lift up others. See the difference it makes. Lift up His name.

Genesis 11:31

*And together they set out from Ur of the
Chaldeans to go to Canaan. But when they came
to Haran, they settled there*

Abraham is considered to be the father of the world's
three largest religions. He is revered by billions of people
as one of the greatest men to ever have lived. But who is he
and why did God call him? At this point in his journey he
still goes by the name his mother gave him: Abram. His
new name of Abraham comes much later.

As far as we know, there was nothing unique or special
about Abram. His father, Terah, was on his way to the
Promised Land: Canaan. But he didn't even get close. The
text says he got as far as Haran, and they settled there.

The striking thing about this story is that in one way or
another, it relates to all of us. Many times God is calling
us to the Promised Land, but we settle. Why do we settle?
Because sometimes it's easier, isn't it? When we settle we
miss out on God's full intent for our lives. Don't give up,
don't settle. Continue until you reach your promised land
in Him.

Isaiah 54:4

Do not be afraid; you will not suffer shame

Israelites are the chosen people of God; there can be no doubt about that. The Bible is replete with Scriptures that testify to that fact. The Bible is also replete with verses that talk about how the nation of Israel continually walked away from God. People wrongly assume that because the Israelites are God's people that they are somehow innately perfect.

What encourages me about God's relationship with Israel is His never-failing love for them. Even though they were unfaithful to Him, He was always faithful to them. Like a husband who caught his wife in adultery, God could have shamed His people. Instead, through the prophet Isaiah He assures them that they will not suffer shame.

Many of us who love God continually fail Him. I'm sure there have been times in your life when you questioned God's actions, maybe even His very existence. Know this—He is faithful despite our actions. Though we may break our covenant with Him, He will never break His with us.

Isaiah 55:1

Come, all you who are thirsty, come to the waters

In the wilderness, water is everything. For those of us who live in developed parts of the world with running water, we can't even begin to imagine what life was like during biblical times. Today if you're thirsty you simply go to your refrigerator and get a nice cold bottle or glass of water.

During the time of the Israelites there was no such luxury. Water was essential to everyday life. Without it you could not water your livestock, your fields, or even sustain your own bodies. It's within this cultural and geographical context that God makes this promise. To the readers of this week's weekly portion, this passage was life! In a dry and dusty part of the world, this passage would have been met enthusiastically by Isaiah's audience.

What about you? Are you thirsty? Are you feeling dry? God's presence is the living water that sustains our spirits. There can be no existence without Him. Come and drink freely from the waters that He offers.

Genesis 12:1

Leave your country, your people, and your
father's household and go to the land
I will show you

Most men don't like to ask for directions, but Abram wasn't even given a hint! Out of the blue God tells Abram to not only leave his father's house but to also leave his country. All God said was that He would lead Abram to a land that He would show him. Talk about your non-specific directions! Abram: "Where shall I go, God?" God: "Over there somewhere." Abram: "Okay." What an odd conversation that must have been.

The text gives no indication that Abram hesitates to obey or challenges the command. He simply gets up and goes. God also told him that He would bless him and make him a great nation. But there was a catch...he had to get up and go.

We all want the blessing of God. We pray for it all the time. But like Abram, are we willing to get out of our comfort zone and follow God no matter what the cost? God will freely bless us, but we must freely obey and trust Him in order to receive the blessing.

Genesis 13:9

If you go to the left, I'll go to the right; if you go to the right, I'll go to the left

Because of Abram's commitment to obeying God, he becomes a blessed man—not only spiritually but financially. In today's economy we think dollars and cents, but in biblical times, your wealth was calculated by your livestock. The biblical description of what Abram had was extensive.

Now Abram's nephew Lot had also acquired great riches. Can you imagine two wealthy related men sharing the same fields to feed their livestock? You would think that one of them would get upset and tell the other to leave.

Instead of arguing, they came to a compromise. Abram said to his nephew, "You go left and I'll go right." What a great act of selflessness and what a great example for us. In our times of blessing we need to be mindful of others. If more people solved their disputes like Abram and Lot, there would be a lot less conflict and tension. Is there a relationship in your life that needs some give-and-take to bring about resolve?

Genesis 14:14

*When Abram heard that his relative had been
taken captive, he ... went in pursuit as far as Dan*

To appreciate this passage you really need to have a map
of Israel handy. Abram is living in the general vicinity of
the Negev Desert, which is way in the south of Israel. The
text says that he went up as far as Dan to retrieve his
nephew. Dan is in the extreme north of the country. It's
actually very close to the modern-day border of Lebanon.

In the previous devotional Abram took the initiative to
help Lot...again in this devotional it is Abram who is
thinking of Lot. The striking thing about this passage is
how far Abram was willing to go to rescue his nephew.

I often wonder how far we would be willing to go to
help someone we knew who was living in distress. I don't
mean how far geographically, but would you drop everything and leave your comfort zone to help someone that
needed you? Let's take the attitude of Abram and go the
distance.

Genesis 15:6

Abram believed the LORD, and He credited it to him as righteousness

We need to understand what a big deal it was that Abram just simply believed the Lord. You need to know his background. Jewish tradition teaches that His father was a professional idol maker, and now he is following the God of Israel. Today's passage tells the story of how Abram believed God for a son in his old age.

In biblical times, having a male heir to inherit your estate was everything. The greatest gift a wife could give her husband was a son to carry on his father's name. Abram is sad because he has no son. The head servant of his house would be next in line.

So Abram cries out to God and expresses his sadness. God tells him that in his old age he will have a son from his own loins that will be the rightful heir. Now Abram could have scoffed at the idea. He could have looked at his situation and said that there was no way such a thing could happen. But instead...He believed God! What has God promised you? Do you feel too young, too old, too (fill in the blank) for God to accomplish it? Believe God, He can do it.

Genesis 17:9

As for you, you must keep my covenant,
you and your descendants after you for the
generations to come

This is the first passage in which God now refers to Abram as Abraham. Up till now Abraham has been having a challenging personal life. His wife, Sarah, can bear him no son, so he is given one of Sarah's maidservants and she conceives. Then the wife who gave the maidservant in the first place later becomes jealous and has Abraham cast her away. Can you imagine such a scenario in our present time? It's a lose-lose situation! His wife was literally telling him to have an affair, so he did, and then she got mad.

The maidservant is crying in the desert when the angel of the Lord finds her and promises her and her son a future. Abraham has yet to have a son by his own wife and God asks him to keep His covenant. The amazing thing is that despite his own personal problems, he chooses to honor God just the same.

When you go through difficult times or when you feel let down, don't turn from God and His promises; instead, run to Him. He will be there waiting for you.

Isaiah 40:31

They will soar on wings like eagles

The context of this passage is one of God's promises to comfort His people. Even though God had delivered His people from the bondage of the Egyptians, Israel really never knew a season of peace. Throughout history until this day, someone is always trying to conquer Israel. I've never fully understood the surrounding nations' obsession with Israel. It is a dry wasteland. Yet over and over again, nations have tried to take it for themselves.

The people had grown weary, they felt like giving up. Then God encouraged His people to not grow weary, but to rise up. Not on their own strength—He would be the very one to lift their heads.

This verse still powerfully applies to us today. Many times in your life you may feel tired, like you just can't go on. The stresses and responsibilities of life can be overwhelming at times. Stop trying to make it on your own steam. Rest in Him; let Him lift you up. If you trust in Him, you can soar on wings like eagles.

Isaiah 41:10

Do not be dismayed, for I am your God

Israel continually grumbled and groaned against both Moses and God during their forty years in the wilderness. As we get into the story of the Exodus, you will begin to see just how much they grumbled. It's amazing that they even made it to the Promised Land. They would get discouraged, and God would provide a miracle. This pattern continued for many years. Even though God provided for them over and over again, they remained dismayed.

Sometimes the constant grumbling evoked the fury of God—He would be pushed to His limits. But other times, like in this passage, He gently and softly assures them of His love and His protection.

What parent among us would not show compassion to our children in their time of need? Those of us who are part of the family of God all share the same loving and faithful Father. Don't let the worries of this world overcome you, but with God's help, you can overcome this world and everything it brings against you.

Genesis 18:27

*Now that I have been so bold as to speak
to the Lord*

How brave are you when you pray? Are you timid in your prayers or do you have the confidence to ask Him for anything? A pattern begins to emerge as you systematically read through the Torah: God doesn't seem to have a problem with people challenging and bargaining with Him. What a foreign thought to those of us who don't come from a Middle Eastern background.

I thought that Abraham was incredibly bold when he spoke up the first time in his request to save the city. But then he just keeps going. I love his catch phrase: "Now that I have been so bold..." What can this teach us about the way we can approach God?

It seems that God was not upset with this bargaining method. However, that doesn't mean that we can belligerently make selfish requests of God. Look at it from a child-parent relationship perspective. Have you ever seen a small child relentlessly asking her mom or dad for what she wants? He is our Father, we are His children. If we ask...we will receive.

Genesis 19:16

For the LORD was merciful to them

I've had the opportunity on many occasions to drive by the modern city of Sodom on the west side of the Dead Sea. It's incredible to imagine what kind of a city was there before God's judgment came down. Sodom and Gomorrah were utterly destroyed because of their sin. The sin was so great that God decided to rain down burning sulfur on the entire region. By morning there was nothing but rising smoke. In the last few moments before the fire was to begin, Lot hesitated. The angels of the Lord grabbed him by the hand and led Lot and the others to safety out of the city.

What a gracious God He is to those who love Him. How many times has the Lord warned us, either about things in our lives that will lead to sin or situations that might put us in physical or spiritual harm?

To those who oppose Him, He is a God to fear. But to those of us who love Him, He is a God to serve in reverent fear. When He reaches out His hand, take hold of it...it may just save your life.

Genesis 20:14

Then Abimelech brought sheep and cattle

Sometimes the Bible contains stories that we just don't understand. This is one of those stories. So often as Christians, we spiritualize the places and people of the Bible so much that we forget how human some of them really were. Abraham is one of those people. Abraham lied about who Sarah was. He told the king that she was his sister instead of telling King Abimelech the truth. The king took her back to his palace, and during the night God rebuked him for taking Sarah.

The next morning Abimelech confronts Abraham about his lie. Abraham tells the king that he acted out of fear and was trying to protect himself. The king was furious because Abraham's lie almost cost Abimelech his entire family.

How many times do people tell a lie with the "best of intentions"? In their minds they're doing it because they wrongly believe that their lie isn't affecting anyone else. From this story we see that's just not the case. We need to tell the truth...always.

Genesis 21:19

*Then God opened her eyes and she saw
a well of water*

This is a heart-wrenching story. Hagar was the maid-servant Sarah had given to Abraham to conceive a child with. Hagar didn't do anything wrong. She didn't go against her master's orders, but in the end she was punished and subsequently banished for her obedience.

Sarah became jealous when Abraham's affections for the boy became obvious. Much to Abraham's sorrow, he had to cast both Hagar and the boy Ishmael away. In today's passage, we find Hagar at the deepest point of desperation. She's given up all hope and in her mind is preparing herself to die. We can't imagine the fear that Hagar as a mother was going through in preparing to watch her child die. Then verse 19 comes along, "Then God opened her eyes and she saw a well of water."

The well didn't magically appear...it had always been there. She couldn't see it in her despair. When you're at the height of your desperation, look to God and let Him open your eyes and show you the well of salvation.

Genesis 22:14

On the mountain of the Lord it will be provided

Abraham waited a hundred years to have an heir born to him. Any parent who has had difficulty in conceiving a child can relate to the sheer joy that Abraham would have experienced when his wife, Sarah, bore him a son. As was the custom in those days, Abraham would have worked closely with Isaac out in the fields passing on what he had learned to his son. So we can only imagine how difficult it would have been for Abraham to obey the command God was about to give him—it was an incredible act of obedience.

First, God asked Abraham to leave his country and his father and now God was asking Abraham to make the most difficult choice any parent could ever imagine. The Lord told Abraham to sacrifice his son. The incredible part of this story is that the text doesn't give any indication that Abraham hesitated . . . he simply obeyed. And in his obedience, God blessed Abraham by providing a substitute sacrifice. When God asks us to do something that seems too much for us to bear, if we act in obedience and with faith God will always provide.

2 Kings 4:3

Go around and ask all your neighbors for empty jars. Don't ask for just a few

Have you ever thought about bargaining with God or trying to change His mind? Can such a thing be done? Moses argued with God when he was told to go to Pharaoh. He was trying to sell himself short by saying that he wasn't a good public speaker. Eventually God agreed to allow Aaron to help. Abraham bargained with God about the number of people necessary to spare the city of Sodom. I was amazed as I read about these stories in the Torah. As Christians we have a whole different understanding of how to approach God.

In this passage, the prophet Elisha tells the widow to go to her neighbors and ask them for jars—but not just a few. During the miracle of self-replenishing oil, the flow stopped because they ran out of jars.

Sometimes we limit God. In our finite way of thinking, we fail to grasp the magnitude of how great God is. Whether your need be small or great today, trust Him to provide.

2 Kings 4:34

*Then he got on the bed and lay upon the boy,
mouth to mouth, eyes to eyes, hands to hands*

Talk about a remarkable story. Talk about an awkward story. Could you imagine this happening today? What would people say or think? The prophet Elisha routinely stayed in a couple's home while traveling in his ministry. Eventually the couple built a spare room for him. In exchange for their kindness, Elisha offers to return the favor by praying for them. They mention that they have no child. He prophesies that they will have a son within a year. A year passes and they have a son.

The boy dies. In agony the wife runs to the prophet for help. An extraordinary chain of events take place, and the boy is raised from the dead. The striking thing from this passage is the amount of passion that this woman exudes in obtaining a miracle for her son.

God wants us to ask, to really ask! He also wants us to believe. The Scriptures are filled with examples of God answering the prayers of the faithful.

Genesis 23:2

(Sarah) died at Kiriath Arba

For any of us who have lost a loved one, we can identify with the profound sadness that Abraham must have gone through at the death of his precious wife, Sarah. We often talk with our spouses about growing old together, and that's exactly what Abraham and Sarah did. Sarah was 127 years old when she died. They accomplished so much together. She was truly a faithful, committed, and supportive wife who stood by his side.

We can only imagine the magnitude of this loss for Abraham. The passage tells us that he mourned and wept over her. He did everything that a husband from that time period was responsible to do. Because he left his home country and found himself in a foreign land, he went out and purchased a cave for family burial. "Life goes on." This was even the case in ancient times. Shortly after Sarah's death, Abraham seeks out a bride for his son, Isaac.

When I lost my dad, I didn't think I'd ever be able to get back to normal. But in reading about Abraham, it's given me the strength to continue on in what God has called me to do. I pray it will be a source of inspiration for you too.

Genesis 24:8

Do not take my son back there

To people of faith, Abraham is always remembered as having been a strong leader and a powerful man of God. What many of us seldom remember is that he was also very human. In today's passage, Abraham is looking for a bride for his son, Isaac. God's instructions were clear—that he was to find a wife for his son from his own clan. I'm sure there were plenty of available women where they lived, yet once again we see that Abraham chooses obedience over convenience.

As the father of two children, I understand Abraham's heart. He wants not just *a* spouse for his son, but he wants *the* spouse that God has for him. From the time before our children were even born, my wife and I were praying for the future spouses of our children. Not only am I so happy in my marriage, but I also know that I married the woman that God had for me. I want the same kind of blessing for my children.

Parents, pray for your child's future spouse. Pray that your child sees past the distractions of this world to the one that God has ordained for him or her.

Genesis 24:51

Take her and go

This passage is about ultimate and absolute trust in God. Imagine the story from the perspective of Rebekah's father, Bethuel. A servant comes into his village and declares that God has sent him to bring back Bethuel's daughter to marry his master's son. Bethuel's response is surprising. Both he and his wife say that this is from the Lord. They agree to the terms of the proposal and send her on her way.

I wonder how we would react if this happened to any of us today. Would we be willing to let our daughter go with someone who seems like a stranger…to give up that control and let God take her to the place He has planned for her?

So maybe a stranger hasn't shown up asking for your daughter's hand in marriage, but is there something in your life that you are holding onto and won't let go of, even though you know God is calling you to let go of it? Is it fear or doubt that holds you back from releasing it to God? If you follow Rebekah's story all the way through, it worked out pretty well for her. When we act in obedience, we can expect blessing.

Genesis 24:63

He went out to the field one evening to meditate

While Abraham was busy planning Isaac's future for him, Isaac decided to set aside some time and do some praying himself. From previous passages, we know that he has come to fully trust his father. If you'll remember, when he was a teenager, his father tied him to an altar and was preparing to sacrifice him. And as far as the text goes, Isaac simply complied. So we know that he trusted his father.

Even in an environment of such trust, Isaac still took the time to go out into the fields on his own and seek out God's will for himself. He could have easily relied on his father's wisdom in the matter, but because of the magnitude of the decision, he needed to get an answer from God for himself.

Sometimes it seems like everyone and his brother knows what's best for you. Everyone has an opinion about what you should become, who you should marry, and myriad other things. Don't dismiss what they say. Take what they say and weigh it against what you feel God is saying to you. Spend time with Him; do what Isaac did... meditate.

Genesis 25:8

Then Abraham breathed his last

The Torah is filled with the stories of many great men of God. Seldom do the Scriptures tell us anything about the birth of these men, but when it comes to their deaths we have the full account. For instance, we're told very little about Abraham. We know his father's name and where he came from, but that's about it. As Abraham's story unfolds, we begin to understand why God chose him.

Abraham's life is one of trust and faith in his God. Although there are many great men in the Torah, God is always referred to as the God of Abraham. By no means was Abraham a perfect man. All we have to do is read his story to find that out. What we learn from his life is that he totally yielded everything and trusted God with his whole life and every aspect of it...all 175 years of it.

I wonder what people would say about me. I wonder what God would say about me. Would I be a man that He would write about? What about you? Are you more interested in what man would say or what God would say? Let's follow Abraham's example and live a life of total devotion to God.

1 Kings 1:6

His father had never rebuked him

This is the story of Adonijah, the fourth son of King David. The text implies that he was raised in such a way that he could do whatever he wanted. Adonijah knew that his father was well advanced in years and that he didn't have much longer to live. It had already been established by solemn proclamation that Solomon would succeed David as king. This news didn't sit well with Adonijah. So he went out and got chariots and horses and gathered all his supporters and began to make sacrifices to inaugurate himself as king.

Bathsheba and the prophet Nathan got wind of this coup and immediately brought it to the king's attention. David seems shocked by the news and puts a plan in motion and brings it to an abrupt stop. What a terrible thing for a son to do to his father. Who raised this kid and why didn't anybody curb this behavior? Verse 6 says that David had never rebuked him by asking him, "Why do you behave as you do?" If you don't like the way your child is behaving or presenting themselves around others, then don't be like King David. Make the time to be there for them and lead them in righteousness.

1 Kings 1:30

*I will surely carry out this very day what I swore
to you by the LORD*

It's common knowledge that King Solomon was the wisest man to ever have lived. I'd like to suggest that King David is a very close second. Read about his life and you'll quickly discover that although he was a great man, he also made a lot of mistakes. But the thing I love about David is that he offers hope for regular people like you and me.

In this passage he's near the end of his life. The text actually says that he was well advanced in his years. Perhaps it was because he was at this stage of his life that those who were against him sought to take advantage of his physical condition. Even in his old age he's quick to respond and put a plan into action. Verse 30 is what stood out to me the most in this entire story. It may have been easier for King David to stay in bed and let somebody else deal with a problem, but he had made a promise before the Lord and he would keep it, even if it killed him.

This is why I think David is a close second. He learned early on that it's better to please God than man.

Genesis 25:20

*Isaac was forty years old when he married
Rebekah*

In ancient times fertility was seen as a blessing from God.
The more children you had, the more blessed you were.
Childbearing was also interpreted as having the favor of
God. So you can imagine that being childless was not only
a huge shame in those times, it also caused others to look
at you funny and talk about you behind your back. People
would wonder why you couldn't have children.

Was there sin in your life? Did you not pray enough? Or
did you marry the wrong person? There were myriad reasons
for being barren. Not only was this hugely embarrassing for
Isaac, but imagine how it made Rebekah feel. After all, her
husband was the son of the great and prolific Abraham.

Wouldn't his father's blessing automatically be transferred to his son? It doesn't work like that in real life, does
it? The text says Isaac prayed. A few verses later Rebekah
is giving birth to twins. Here's the catch...twenty years
had passed. Sometimes God takes a little longer than we
would like to answer prayer. The truth is, He is never late;
His timing is perfect.

Genesis 26:12

Reaped a hundredfold

Earlier we read about how fertility was a sign of the favor of the Lord. Another way to measure His blessing was by the amount of livestock you had. Still another method was by the size of your harvest from the fields. This passage says that Isaac became so rich that even the mighty Philistines were jealous—so jealous, in fact, that they asked him to leave the area.

Perhaps you're reading this today and wish you were as rich as Isaac. I'm sure having money is nice, but it's not without its problems either. Have you ever had either an unexpected blessing or a sudden acquisition of something valuable? One of two things will happen. Those who call themselves your friends will either rejoice with you or become bitter, because in their minds it should have happened to them and not you.

True friends rejoice when their friends succeed. That's why it is so important to surround yourself with people who love you for who you are, not what you have. So today I pray that God will richly bless you with true friends.

Genesis 26:22

He moved on from there and dug another well

Everyone has their own Bible hero, someone they look up to because the biblical character has a certain trait or quality that people either identify with or wish they had. I have to say that Isaac is quickly becoming one of my new heroes. His level of patience is unbelievable. Those who know me would be quick to say that I could use a little more patience in my life when it comes to waiting for something to happen.

I don't know how I would react if it were me in today's passage. Isaac's father, Abraham, had legally and legitimately dug wells for his livestock. Isaac was within his rights to claim and use said wells. Each time he reopened the wells that were legally his, someone opposed him. Sometimes they simply stopped them up by filling them with dirt. Not once, not twice, but this happened on four different occasions.

This is what really impresses me—the text gives no indication that Isaac got mad! He simply moved on to the next one and tried again until he finally reached an area where no one challenged him. May God grant us all such patience to live in peace.

Genesis 26:28

*We saw clearly that the L*ORD *was with you*

Knowing who your friends are is very important, but in biblical times, knowing who your enemies were was even more important. Yesterday we read about how Isaac kept moving from well to well until he found a place of peace. It's amazing to me how quick King Abimelech was in going to see Isaac in his newfound place of peace. You can imagine Isaac's surprise when he saw the king coming.

This time Isaac isn't so pleasant and quite frankly asks him what he is doing there. Isaac boldly says to the king that while Isaac lived in his territory the king was hostile to him. So what on earth could he want from Isaac now?

The king says to him that it was clear that the Lord was with Isaac. "Why can't we all just get along?" is what the king was saying. It's amazing how, when some people find out that you are blessed, all of a sudden they want to be your friend. Isaac decides that a friend is better than a foe. Are there any foes out there that you need to make into an ally?

Genesis 28:4

Take possession of the land

Often we pray to the God of Abraham, Isaac, and Jacob. But what do we really know of the men whose names we use in our prayers? In the passages leading up to today's reading we are introduced to Jacob and his twin brother, Esau. I've read their story several times during my journey of faith, but this time something really stood out to me…Jacob was no saint.

Sometimes we wrongfully elevate the people in the Bible to a status of something perfect—like they can do no wrong. Read the passage; Jacob did wrong, lots of wrong. In fact, if people in our churches today did what he did, we would deny them membership and probably have them excommunicated. That's why I both love and trust the Bible. It doesn't try to paint everyone with a flawless brush. It's filled with real people and their very real problems.

Despite everything Jacob did, he was still able to inherit the promises of God—that he would take possession of the land that was promised to him. That's why I both love and trust my God.

Malachi 1:6

Where is the honor due me?

In some cultures, honor is the most important thing. Not money, not power, not fame...but honor. The honoring of one's parents in many cultures is paramount. I know in my own Portuguese culture that that is the case. During the biblical period it was the same. The honoring of your parents was sometimes the difference between being blessed or being cursed, receiving the inheritance or not.

In fact, honor made God's top ten list, the Ten Commandments. It's number five. It comes before murder, adultery, and stealing. Wow! Have you ever thought about that before? I don't know if many people have. And so, for many of us, when thinking about actions that please God, honor doesn't make our top ten list either.

In this passage God asks, where is the honor due Him? That's a big question. How do we honor God? The truth is that there is no one way to do that. But here's an important one: we honor Him in everything we do and say. We should strive to live a life of righteousness while asking Him to guide us by His Holy Spirit. We need to guard our hearts, our minds, and our mouths.

Malachi 2:7

For the lips of a priest ought to preserve knowledge

The prophet Malachi is usually only quoted by people when they want to talk about finances. But did you know there was a lot more to his writings? Malachi was written soon after the return of the Jewish people from the Babylonian exile. The Jewish people had been through an incredibly difficult period in their history. Their Temple had been destroyed and they were taken captive.

Now that they were back in the land of Israel, they had to start over from scratch. This brought a tremendous amount of apathy from the people. Imagine that you had spent years building an intricate puzzle and then someone came along and threw all the pieces on the floor. How excited would you be to begin the rebuilding process? Now you know how the Jewish people felt.

The Lord was trying to motivate his people through the prophet Malachi. He was encouraging the priests as well. He wanted them to teach the people His decrees that had been forgotten. God wants you to use your mouth to declare His great message.

Genesis 28:15

*I am with you and will watch over you
wherever you go*

In this passage Jacob is running for his life. His mother, Rebekah, told him to go back to the country of her ancestry and that there he would find a new life.

Somewhere along the journey he decides to settle down for the night. He grabs a stone for a pillow and goes off to sleep. He got anything but a normal night's sleep. During the night he had a dream that most of us know today as "Jacob's ladder." In fact it was a stairway, and at the top of the stairway was the Lord Himself.

In the dream God made some very powerful promises to Jacob. For instance, that he would inherit the land God promised to Abraham and Isaac. But I think the promise Jacob needed to hear the most was that God was with him and would watch over him, no matter where he would go. A comforting promise in light of why he was running away in the first place. If God meant it for Jacob, He meant it for you also. God is with you, He is on your side, and He is watching over you too.

Genesis 29:20

So Jacob served seven years

There are some powerful and life-changing stories in the Bible. Then there are stories like this one about Jacob and his wife Rachel...I mean Leah...hang on a second!

The passage describes the story of how Jacob was in love with Laban's younger daughter, Rachel. In exchange for her hand in marriage, Jacob pledged to work seven years for Laban. It also says that the seven years only felt like a few days because of his great love for her. How romantic. Sometime during the evening, Laban replaced Rachel with his older daughter, Leah. When Jacob woke up the next morning he was furious because he had been deceived. In the end he gets Rachel back, but it costs him an additional seven years of service. Fourteen years in all.

Although Jacob was upset, he never acted on that anger. Instead he sought a solution, which in this case was to work for seven more years. How do we handle ourselves when we are deceived? Do we react out of anger, or do we seek out the best solution?

Genesis 30:1

Give me children, or I'll die

We have already established in previous devotionals that preserving the family bloodline was everything in biblical times. Jacob now has two wives, Rachel and Leah. Leah knew that Jacob loved Rachel more, so she was very jealous and, as you can imagine, also very insecure. God had mercy on her and granted her four children with Jacob. She thought to herself that surely now Jacob would love her because she had borne him four healthy males to carry on the family name.

Yet Jacob still loved Rachel more. Although Leah was ecstatic with all the children she bore, Rachel, on the other hand, was not. For the first time it is now Rachel who is jealous. She is humiliated because she cannot give her husband any children. In haste she gives him a maidservant with whom to have a child. It's like Sarah and Hagar all over again.

So often we get ahead of God and act on our own. How many times have we been waiting on God for something, but instead of waiting we take matters into our own hands? Sometimes we need to wait for God, because His timing will always be perfect.

Genesis 31:2

*And Jacob noticed that Laban's attitude toward
him was not what it had been*

Jacob had been working very hard for many years now for
his father-in-law, Laban. The text never mentions, not even
once, that Jacob was unhappy or that he complained. He
just got up every day and went to work. That was not the
case for Laban's sons. The sons told their father that Jacob
was stealing everything and would one day leave Laban
empty handed. Shortly thereafter Jacob began to notice
that Laban's attitude toward him was beginning to change.

Maybe Laban wasn't as patient or he made Jacob work
longer days. The point is that Laban started to treat him
differently because of what his sons said. That's what I
want to focus on today. What we hear tends to affect how
we think, and in turn affects how we act. We can be in a
relationship or friendship for a long time, but if we hear
something about that person, even if we can't verify it, we
begin to see that person through that tainted lens. Don't
listen to or participate in gossip. Nothing good will come
of it. Proverbs 16:28 says that "a gossip separates close
friends."

Genesis 31:50

*Remember that God is a witness
between you and me*

This passage is one of the greatest proofs that God watches out for the righteous. From the text we are told that Laban was continually trying to cheat Jacob out of what he had rightly and honestly worked for. Laban changed Jacob's wage ten times, and I'm pretty sure they weren't raises.

God was blessing Jacob and the livestock was multiplying...remember that livestock was the currency of the day. To limit Jacob's income Laban would say that Jacob could only keep the goats that were born speckled, so God caused all the goats to be born speckled. Then Laban said Jacob could only keep the goats that were born streaked, so God caused all the goats to be born with streaks. That's not even the crazy part about the story, this is: Jacob stayed and kept working hard anyway because he had given Laban his word. Talk about a wow!

I don't think any of us have been cheated anywhere near the degree that Jacob was. Keep working with honesty and integrity, because the only one who matters is watching...God.

Hosea 11:8

My heart is changed within me;
all my compassion is aroused

Hosea was quite the prophet. In the opening verses of his writings he is told by God to go and marry an adulterous wife—something that was contrary to what God had said before. So why the change? Why such an unorthodox command? To understand the Bible, sometimes we need to take in the local culture. God uses symbolism and comparisons on a regular basis throughout the Scriptures.

God asked Hosea to marry an unfaithful woman because he was sending a message to Israel: though you are unfaithful, I will still keep my covenant to you. Although alarming, it is a striking example of God's love not only for Israel, but for us also.

This reading for the week is beautiful because although Israel deserved to be punished and abandoned, God's love could never let that happen. That should give us tremendous comfort. He loves us not because we are perfect, but because we are His.

Hosea 12:7

*The merchant uses dishonest scales;
he loves to defraud*

Everybody wants to get a good deal. Who wants to pay full price when you can get it on sale? There's absolutely nothing wrong with being frugal and a wise shopper. But how far are you willing to go to get a good deal? That's what today's reading is all about. Merchants were starting to tip the scales in their favor. Customers were getting charged more but they were getting less. This passage is all about honesty and acquiring things in an honest manner. Some people think that as long as they don't get caught that it's not wrong.

At times it seems as though those who deceive and scheme are getting ahead. They have nicer cars, bigger houses, and on and on. Many of them love to brag and tell of their ill-gotten gain.

They may get away with it for a while, or they may never get caught. But it's not your place to get mad or jealous. Do all that you can do to live right and please God. In the end, you're the only person whose actions you can control and have to account for.

Genesis 32:9

Then Jacob prayed

Jacob had been living in the land of his ancestors and had done very well for himself. He had put off going back to the land God had promised him long enough. He knew that going back would mean facing the consequences of what he had done that had caused him to flee in the first place. He would have to come face to face with his twin brother, Esau, whom he had cheated those many years before.

He was afraid because his servants had reported to him that Esau was coming with four hundred men! He could only assume the worst. Surely his brother wasn't coming with his army to attend a family reunion. What could Jacob do? He tried to soften the meeting by sending ahead large amounts of livestock to soften the blow.

It's amazing how many times we resort to every other possible measure to solve a problem before turning to the Lord in prayer. Jacob tried every way he could think of to appease his brother, but in the end he did the right thing—he prayed. Don't make God your last resort; he should be your first option.

Genesis 32:26

I will not let you go unless you bless me

Jacob is still anticipating the meeting with his brother. In preparation for the meeting he sends his family across the river Jabbok. He wants to spend some time alone. Maybe he wants to go over in his mind what he will say when they finally meet. Maybe he wants to plan an exit strategy. The point is, he needs some time on his own. However, the opposite happens. The text very casually informs us that a man wrestles with Jacob all night.

The man turns out to be the angel of the Lord. That's another way of saying that it was God. They wrestle through the night until the angel touches Jacob's hip. Then something momentous happens: his name is changed to Israel.

I can relate to Jacob in this passage. Before a big event, whether it's a speaking engagement or a television appearance, I like to get away on my own and just think things through. And like Jacob, sometimes I wrestle with God about what to say or how to say it. If we stay the course and wrestle it through, then there is a blessing waiting for us.

Genesis 33:3

And bowed down to the ground

The moment of truth had arrived. After all those many years of running, after all the gifts and after all the anticipation, it happened—he came face to face with his brother. Jacob looked up and saw his brother coming with his army of four hundred men. In fear, he began to divide the children up among his wives and servants. When his brother got within speaking distance, he fell down to the ground on his face seven different times as a sign of submission.

What happened next gave Jacob the shock of his life. I'm sure he had mentally prepared for the worst. His brother would kill him. Maybe he would receive some kind of a beating. At the very least a severe scolding. But nothing...

Esau threw his arms around his brother and received him as if nothing had ever happened. I'm sure Jacob was both relieved and stunned by this welcome. Esau was happy to see his brother and was so blessed to see all the wealth that God had given him. Sometimes we imagine the worst-case scenario, but the truth is that God has been working in the background in our favor!

Genesis 33:10

For to see your face is like seeing the face of God

Have you ever been to a family reunion? I think everyone has that one relative that they dread seeing at those reunions. Maybe it's a judgmental person who has nothing but negative things to say about everyone on the planet. Maybe it's the family gossip who talks incessantly about everyone's problems. Whoever it may be, you can relate to Jacob's apprehension.

But when they met, it was like no time had passed and no negative experience had taken place. God had been working on Jacob's heart for decades. He had taught him to live with integrity while working for Laban. Do you remember the actions that led to Jacob fleeing from his brother? There was deception and cheating. Interesting, isn't it—what he had done to his brother was also done to him by Laban.

Here's the catch . . . God had been working on Jacob, but what Jacob didn't count on was that God was also at work in his brother. Don't fear the worst. The same God who changes you also changes others.

Genesis 35:2

Get rid of the foreign gods

Things are finally starting to look up for Jacob. He has been restored to his brother after many years of running. He's back on track and heading toward the land that was promised to him through Abraham and Isaac. God called a meeting with Jacob at the placed called Bethel. That's the place where Jacob fled to when he was running from Esau. Now that the reconciliation was complete, it seemed that the Lord was bringing Jacob full circle.

But there were a few conditions Jacob and his family had to follow before they could go up to Bethel. They had to get rid of all their foreign gods, purify themselves, and change their clothes. The text so casually mentions getting rid of their foreign gods. No one seemed surprised that they had them, they just had to get rid of them before they went up to meet with God.

I wonder how many of us are casually carrying around foreign gods? I don't mean little statues in a purse or briefcase, but in our hearts and minds. Exodus 20:3 says, "You shall have no other gods before me."

Genesis 35:10

Your name will be Israel

Jacob and his family begin the trek to Canaan to meet with God at the place He called Bethel. For reasons the text doesn't explain, this is the place where God seems to meet with Jacob. When they arrive at the place, God begins to speak to Jacob almost immediately.

The first thing that happens is that God blesses Jacob and changes his name to Israel. In Hebrew, *Israel* means "prince with God." The Lord then proceeds to reaffirm all of His promises to Jacob that he had previously made to Abraham and Isaac. The promise was twofold. First, that he would inherit the land of Canaan, which is the modern-day State of Israel. Second, that a great nation with kings would come from him.

Name changes in the Bible occur when people either do great things or they are about to do great things. We saw this earlier with Abraham. Names in the biblical period weren't just a way to identify *who* you were, but many times they were a way to identify *what* you were! Be open to changes in your life because God is guiding you into the destiny He has for you.

Obadiah 1:15

As you have done, it will be done to you

As I write this devotional I have conflicting thoughts. This prophecy in Obadiah is against the kingdom of Edom, the descendants of Esau—Jacob's twin brother. I'm conflicted because only three days ago we read about Jacob and Esau's heart-wrenching reunion, where forgiveness was in great abundance. Today's passage is about the impending judgment on Esau's house. The line that jumped out at me was verse 15, where it says, "As you have done, it will be done to you."

Initially Esau showed compassion and forgiveness, but later on his descendants turned back to violence and vengeance. It's in this context that the prophecy is made. To modernize the statement, it's the old "what goes around comes around" clause.

This should really cause us to reflect on the way we treat others and the values we pass on to our children and other loved ones. If you want mercy, then show mercy. If you want grace, then show grace.

Genesis 37:9

I had another dream

The story of Joseph sounds like something straight out of a Hollywood movie, except this is real life. What a story. Over the next few days we'll be tracking with Joseph to see how his story unfolds. But let's start from the beginning. In terms of probability of being disliked by his brothers, he has everything against him. The text says that Joseph was his father's favorite son and to declare that, he had a richly ornamented robe made for him to wear.

I'm sure this didn't sit well with his older brothers. On top of everything, Joseph came back from the fields and brought a bad report to Jacob about the other brothers. In other words, he was probably snitching on something they were doing while they were supposed to be working. To make matters worse, he proceeds to tell his brothers about a dream he had in which all of them were bowing down and worshiping him—that's a formula for trouble!

There's nothing wrong when God gives you a dream that elevates you above others—some are called to be presidents and kings. The key is having the wisdom of knowing who to tell and who not to.

Genesis 37:17

So Joseph went after his brothers

Joseph's brothers were pretty bothered by the two dreams he had, and I'm sure it drove a wedge between them and made their relationship even more unstable. Once again his father sent him out to spy on the older boys.

The brothers saw Joseph coming in the distance and let's just say they weren't overjoyed. The brothers actually recommended killing him and throwing him into a pit. They planned to tell their father that he had been devoured by a wild animal. Here comes that dreamer, they said to themselves.

Only one brother stood up and defended Joseph. Reuben recommended just throwing him into the pit, not actually harming him. He did this because at the end of the day he was planning to go help Joseph out. There was a lot of peer pressure going on, but Reuben chose to speak out. I know it can be difficult to speak out against peer pressure sometimes, but in the end we have to stand up for what is right, no matter what others will say or think about us.

Genesis 37:26

*What will we gain if we kill our brother and
cover up his blood?*

What a touching sentiment from Judah—yeah, right!
I'm only being so sarcastic with this part of the story
because for those of you who know how it ends, it makes
Joseph's behavior later on all that more powerful.

Instead of killing him, they decided to sell him for
twenty shekels to some spice traders. They didn't know
where he would end up or how he would be treated. All
they knew was that this "dreamer" would no longer be
their problem.

They kept Joseph's special robe that was custom made
by their father. They killed a goat and dipped the robe in it
and presented it to their father for verification. Jacob
immediately recognized the robe as Joseph's and he wept
bitterly and was inconsolable.

Passing on your problem to someone else isn't necessarily going to get rid of it. Those kinds of things have a
tendency to come back to haunt you.

Genesis 38:26

She is more righteous than I

After Joseph was sold into slavery, Judah leaves to make his own life. He meets a woman, falls in love, and gets married. Eventually they have three sons together. Then as they grow up the oldest also falls in love and marries a woman named Tamar. Judah's firstborn son, however, was so wicked that the Lord put him to death.

As was the custom in those days, it was the next eldest brother's responsibility to marry his brother's wife and carry on the family name. The second son was also wicked and was put to death. The third son was far too young, so Tamar was sent away to wait for him to grow up. Judah happened to have business in the area where his daughter-in-law Tamar was. She dressed up like a temple prostitute, and Judah approached her and slept with her. She became pregnant. She took certain items from him as collateral.

Judah was preparing to condemn her to death because of her great sin, but then she presented the items she had taken from him. He quickly dismissed the charges. Be careful of condemning others, your own sin has a funny way of coming back to you.

Genesis 39:2

The LORD was with Joseph

Have you ever heard the expression, "If life gives you lemons, make lemonade"? I think Joseph could have invented that phrase. Joseph is such an amazing person. His brothers traded him for a few shekels, then those who bought him sold him into slavery into the service of Potiphar.

While he was there he worked hard. The text says that the Lord was with Joseph and that he prospered. In fact, he excelled so greatly that Potiphar put him in charge of his entire house. Potiphar concerned himself with nothing except the food he ate. The passage goes on to say that Joseph was well built and handsome, and he caught the eye of Potiphar's wife. She tried to seduce him, but Joseph refused.

I love what he did; he didn't walk quietly away from her. He didn't try to sneak out while she was busy or sleeping. He looked her right in the eye and then he ran! That's what we need to do when temptation comes our way. Don't let it taunt you, just run.

Genesis 40:23

He forgot him

First of all, in spying on his brothers, Joseph did what his father, Jacob, asked him to do. All that did was get him sold into slavery. Then he honors God by working so hard for Potiphar that he gets promoted to the highest position in the house. Then he honors Potiphar by not succumbing to his wife's advances, and somehow he still gets the short end of the stick by being sent to prison because Potiphar's wife wrongfully accused Joseph.

I don't know about you, but at this point I would not be in the mood to be nice to others. I would just want to sit in that prison cell and be left alone. But not Joseph; he allows God to use him no matter where he is. The chief cupbearer had a troublesome dream, and Joseph gave him the interpretation. It was good news. Within three days the king would call for him and restore him to his former position.

All Joseph asks for in exchange is that the cupbearer remembers Joseph's case when he sees the king. One of the saddest lines in the Bible…he forgot him! When things are going well for you, don't forget about the plight of others. Do what you can to help those around you. It's our responsibility.

Amos 3:2

You only have I chosen

The book of Amos is one of those books that we know is in the Bible, but it doesn't get read all that often. Amos is one of the minor prophets, and his book has been treated that way. But God chose for it to be part of the weekly reading system. That's good enough testimony for me that we should pay extra attention to it.

Amos was not a career prophet like Isaiah or Jeremiah as well as many others. He refers to himself as a farmer, more specifically, a sycamore-fig farmer. Yet God called him to bring His message to the northern part of the nation. You don't have to be a professional minister to be a minister! You can work in an office or drive a taxi—it really doesn't matter.

The text is dealing with judgment against Israel. Sounds familiar, doesn't it? Although God says, "You only have I chosen," He also says, "I will punish you." Just because they were chosen by God, it didn't exempt them from consequences. Even if we belong to God, we still have to give an account for our actions.

Genesis 41:8

*So he sent for all the magicians and
wise men of Egypt*

The opening statement of this week's reading is very sad: "When two full years had passed." That's how long Joseph sat in prison for being falsely accused by Potiphar's wife, and since the cupbearer had forgotten about Joseph. The passage says that Pharaoh had a troubling dream. So he did what he would normally do, he turned to his magicians and those who were considered to be wise among the Egyptians.

Much to Pharaoh's dismay, no one was able to interpret the dream for him. All of a sudden the cupbearer has a flashback to two years earlier, to Joseph, the Hebrew prisoner who had interpreted his dream correctly. It took him long enough! I guess better late than never.

He approaches Pharaoh and tells him about Joseph. Pharaoh sends for Joseph and asks him if he can interpret his dream. I love Joseph's answer: "I cannot do it, but God will give Pharaoh the answer he desires." Joseph was quick to give God all the glory for his gift. What an example for us.

Genesis 41:41

*I hereby put you in charge of the whole land
of Egypt*

Justice had finally been served! Joseph's name had been restored, and by no less than the highest authority in all Egypt—Pharaoh himself. Joseph was quick to implement the plan that God had shown him. The passage says that under Joseph's leadership the land was so blessed that they stopped keeping records because it was too difficult to record everything.

His prison uniform was exchanged for robes of fine linen. I wonder if Joseph ever looked into the mirror and caught a glimpse of what he had before all this tragedy had befallen him. Everything that had been taken away was about to be restored to him. Even Joseph wasn't aware of all that was about to happen—that God would cause his dream to be fulfilled, that he would be restored and reconciled to his brothers and father.

There are so many lessons for us to glean from Joseph's life. He always kept a positive attitude, he never gave up, and he was always careful to give God the glory.

Genesis 42:1

Why do you just keep looking at each other?

Sometimes people are so quick to point out the problem, but seldom do they seek out the solution. Jacob was a solution seeker. He tells his sons to go to Egypt and buy grain. Stop talking about it, load up the cargo, and get down there to buy some food—good fatherly advice.

Joseph's brothers had no idea what was about to happen! They thought they were going out on a routine grocery run—buy the food, come home, get on with life. Boy, were they in for the surprise of their lives! Joseph himself was overseeing the sales of grain to foreigners. When his brothers arrived, they assumed the proper position when you come into the presence of someone as powerful as Joseph, you get down on your knees and bow.

Joseph immediately recognized his brothers, even after all those years. He didn't let on like he knew them and spoke harshly to them. I wonder if Joseph thought about his dream in that moment—that one day his brothers would bow before him. Stay faithful to God; dreams do come true.

Genesis 42:21

*Surely we are being punished because
of our brother*

No, really? We know that Joseph's brothers were in for the surprise of their lives, but what about Joseph? Have you ever considered what it must have been like for him to see his brothers after all those years? Did he think about what they did when he couldn't sleep at night? Did he play it over and over again, night after night, in prison? I'm sure most us would. But the text says that when he saw his brothers he remembered his dreams.

At first it seems that Joseph is treating them harshly to exact revenge; who could blame him? But the truth is that he was setting a plan in motion—a plan to bring his entire family down to Egypt. He put them in prison for three days and then demanded that they leave one brother behind while the rest go back home to bring Jacob and Benjamin back to Egypt for Joseph to see.

It took all these events to get the brothers thinking their past actions were coming back to them. We may forget what we did, we may even get on with our lives, but unresolved actions are a ticking time bomb.

Genesis 43:26

And they bowed down before him to the ground

Let's go back to the beginning of Joseph's journey. The only thing he did to invoke his brothers' hatred for him was to be born. From the story's opening there is no indication that Joseph was a bad kid or that he had done anything malicious toward his brothers. His brothers simply had an issue with him because he was Daddy's favorite. That was all the reason the other boys needed.

Was it his fault he was born? What it his fault that God gave him those dreams? Of course not, yet he was mistreated because of it. Do you remember how angry and insulted the brothers were when Joseph told them his dream that one day they would all bow down to him? "How arrogant of him," they must have thought. "Who does this guy think he is?" No wonder they were so mad.

All the while, though, God was in the background orchestrating the events that would ultimately lead toward the fulfillment of the dream that He had given Joseph. Don't give up hope. God is working things out for you. Trust him every day.

Genesis 44:1

Fill the men's sacks with as much food as
they can carry

How far would you be willing to go in order to carry out a plan—even one with the best of intentions? Would you go as far as Joseph did? First, he threw them in jail for a few nights to mull over their actions. Then he asked them to go back home and bring their youngest brother with them.

Just as he is set to send them back to get their father, Joseph sets them up by hiding his personal cup in the sack of the youngest one, Benjamin. The passage is very clear in indicating that since the "death" of Joseph, Benjamin is now Jacob's favorite son.

It seems cruel that he would hold the youngest son back. His thinking was that it would ensure his father would come to Egypt.

Sometimes things happen to us that we don't understand. I know Joseph's brothers were both confused and upset at what was happening to them. In the end it all worked out and their relationships were restored. Do you trust God to do what is right in your life? I hope so.

1 Kings 3:16

*Now two prostitutes came to the king and
stood before him*

The purpose of 1 Kings was to preserve the historical legacy of the Jewish nation. That's why it's a little surprising that one of the first stories in this book to demonstrate King Solomon's wisdom involves two prostitutes and two babies born out of wedlock.

These two women lived together and eventually they each gave birth to a son within three days of each other. The first woman claimed that the second woman's baby died during the night and that she changed the position of the babies to make it look like the first woman's baby died. The matter was brought before the king. He asked for a sword to cut the living child in two to be shared by both women. The first woman said no and told the king to give the child to the second woman. The second woman said for the king to go ahead. His wise ruling was that the first woman was the mother of the child and gave her the baby.

What an incredible story. May we all govern our lives with the wisdom of King Solomon!

Genesis 44:30

Whose life is closely bound up with the boy's life

At this stage of Joseph's plan, his brothers can no longer bear this cruel game. Judah stood up and recounted all that Joseph had required of them and how they had carried out all of his commands no matter how personally difficult it was for them.

Joseph was threatening to keep Benjamin behind while all the other brothers went back to get their father, Jacob. Judah's point is that Jacob's life is so tied to his youngest son's life that if the brothers appear without him, Jacob will assume he is dead and that will be too much for Jacob and he will die. I wonder what was going through Judah's mind. Surely the thought of delivering the news of Joseph's death all those years ago made him feel guilty enough. He couldn't bear the thought of his father thinking that another one of his sons had died. Judah offered himself to stay in place of Benjamin.

Even though it may come at great cost, sometimes we must put others first, even at great personal sacrifice.

Genesis 45:3

*But his brothers were not able to answer him,
because they were terrified at his presence*

The story of Joseph could easily be turned into a Hollywood major motion picture. It has all the elements to produce a blockbuster hit, including action and drama. One of the climaxes of this story is found in today's passage: Joseph finally reveals himself to his brothers.

I know that it was Judah who stood up and made the plea to stay instead of their younger brother, Benjamin, but you have to wonder what it was doing to Joseph. All those years in prison and in Pharaoh's service, he must have thought about how much his father was hurting, believing that his son was dead. All that pain he had been holding onto for all those years rose up in that moment. He couldn't cause his father to think even for a moment that Benjamin was dead.

When we have been deceived for a long time and the truth is finally revealed, it can be a shocking, even a bit scary. Are you being deceived? Ask God to show you.

Genesis 45:8

*So then, it was not you who sent me here,
but God*

How could Joseph say such a thing? It was his brothers who threw him into a pit and then sold him to spice traders. It was the spice traders who sold him as a servant to Potiphar, and because of Potiphar's wife he ended up in prison for two years.

It was because of them that the cupbearer forgot about him, and it was because of that he was eventually brought before Pharaoh to interpret his dream, and it was because of that he was placed second in command in all the land.

And it was because Joseph governed with such wisdom that the entire land of Egypt was filled with food during the most severe famine in the region. And it was because they had so much food that his brothers came down to Egypt. And it was because he was in charge of selling the food that he saw his brothers, and because...

So you see, it *was* God who brought Joseph to Egypt. In all that you go through, trust God. He knows the end from the beginning.

Genesis 45:20

*Never mind about your belongings, because the
best of all Egypt will be yours*

Genesis is clear when it says that Joseph had found favor
in the eyes of Pharaoh, but had you considered how far
that favor went? Even though Joseph had been convicted
of a crime and thrown into prison, it didn't stop Pharaoh
from restoring Joseph. He exalted Joseph to second in
command in all of Egypt. That sounds really great, but it
also meant that Joseph was now above Potiphar—the one
who put him into prison in the first place. Talk about
awkward staff meetings!

Joseph is preparing to send his brothers back to Canaan
to bring their father with them and Pharaoh gets wind of
this reunion. His reaction is somewhat out of character for
a man in his position. He lavishes Joseph's family with
everything they need for the journey home. Then he says
to leave all their stuff at home because they will receive
the best of Egypt upon their return.

When God redeems you, he not only gives you everything back, He gives you the very best.

Genesis 46:3

*Do not be afraid to go down to Egypt, for I will
make you into a great nation there*

As a father, I can't imagine what Jacob was going through
back home in Canaan. Up till now the story has been
focused on Joseph and his brothers, but what about Jacob?
You have to remember that there was no way to stay in
touch or find out what was happening. When his sons set
out for Egypt, it would most likely be weeks before he
would see them again, if he would ever see them again
at all.

In our modern age where every imaginable method of
communication is available to us in the palm of our
hands, we can't relate to the loneliness and anxiety Jacob
was going through. You know how paranoid you get when
the person you're calling doesn't answer the phone or
doesn't reply to your text…imagine Jacob. So he waited.
One day as he was waiting the Lord spoke to him. Jacob
may not have had a cell phone or email, but he had God!

The Lord prepared him for the journey to Egypt. Technology is good, but God is better!

Genesis 47:27

Now the Israelites settled in Egypt in the region of Goshen

Have you ever experienced divine favor? I mean something happened to you that you were not planning or expecting, but when it did, you knew it was God's blessing. I'm not talking about getting a good parking space at the mall. I've had the privilege of traveling to many countries around the world. I usually fly at my own expense, so I always book economy. But once or twice, I was upgraded to first class, and that was nice.

I might think that's a pretty cool thing, some might even call it divine favor because I was traveling doing the Lord's work. But that pales in comparison to what God did for Joseph's family when they arrived in Egypt. Like most foreigners, they would normally be given a place to dwell where the locals wouldn't want to live. It's not policy to give away your best land to foreigners.

Yet, that's exactly what God did. They were given the area of Goshen to dwell in—the most lush and fertile region. God knows how to take care of His children.

Ezekiel 37:22

*There will be one king over all of them and they
will never again be divided*

Ezekiel was written during the Babylonian exile—one of
the worst periods in Jewish history. The city had been
ransacked, the Holy Temple was destroyed, and the people
were exiled from their land. It was a sad time for the Jewish people, and a time that affects Israel to this day.

Those who were exiled to Babylon were looking for
guidance and comfort from God. Israel has been through
too many trials to mention here. But between this first
exile and subsequent destruction of the Temple came a
second and final exile under Roman occupation and then
Herod's Second Temple was destroyed for good. Not to
mention the Crusades and the Holocaust...Israel was
looking for some good news.

In today's reading we see they find it! God promises to
rule over them as King and to never divide their land
again. To a people who were constantly divided, this
prophecy was a welcome one. God keeps His word. So
whatever He has promised you, rest assured that He will
keep and fulfill it.

Genesis 48:11

I never expected to see your face again, and now
God has allowed me to see your children too

This is such a beautiful and heartwarming passage. It shows us two of the greatest characteristics of God: His compassion and mercy. Jacob had been through so much in his life. Remember when he fell in love with Rachel and worked seven years for her, only to be cheated and have to work seven more? Remember all the challenges he faced when he was preparing to meet his brother, Esau?

Imagine how heartbroken he was to find out that his son Joseph was torn to pieces by a wild beast. And finally, he loses his wife too. What a life! In all our readings of Jacob, he always blessed God. He never thought he would see his son Joseph again. Yet not only did he see Joseph, but he saw Joseph's position in Egypt, second only to Pharaoh. What a proud moment that must have been for him.

And now he gets the icing on the cake—he gets to see and bless the grandchildren that he never even knew he had. We serve a great and merciful God.

Genesis 48:17

*When Joseph saw his father placing his right
hand on Ephraim's head he was displeased*

During biblical times, the birth order of males decided who would carry on the family blessing and inherit the father's land and money. Firstborns were highly respected because logically they would be next in line to rule and govern the family.

That's what makes this passage so interesting. Joseph brought his two sons before his father, Jacob. He was looking to have them blessed and recognized for their future roles in the family. Joseph even lined the boys up in the right order for Jacob because Jacob's eyes were failing.

Even though his eyes were failing, he told Joseph that he was laying his hands on the right boy. Everyone expected that the older boy would rule, but God had chosen the younger one.

Sometimes we expect God to move in a certain way because we think we have Him all figured out. Instead of getting angry like Joseph, yield to God in His decision.

Genesis 49:28

*This is what their father said to them when he
blessed them, giving each the blessing
appropriate to him*

When you think about Jacob blessing his sons, like me,
you're probably thinking happy thoughts. Isn't it nice that
on his deathbed he gathers all his sons and is ready to tell
them how wonderful they all are and how proud he is of
all of them?

You might be shocked by what he actually says to them.
Instead of it being some "blessfest," he calls it like it is. He
praises some for the good they had done and he rebukes
the others for the evils they had committed.

One son he calls a lion and can't say enough good
things about him. He compares another to a lazy donkey.
To another, Jacob says he is like a serpent by the roadside.

His sons couldn't expect to live like they did and then
have it all forgotten when their father was ready to hand
out the blessings. Like Jacob loved his sons, God loves us
dearly, but our rewards, or lack thereof, will be deter-
mined by how we live our lives.

Genesis 50:1

*Joseph threw himself upon his father
and wept over him and kissed him*

I'm gonna be open and honest with you from the very outset of today's devotional. This is by far the most difficult one out of all 378 that I wrote for this book. This one hits too close to home for me.

At 11:31 p.m. EST, on October 22, 2008, my dad died after a nineteen-month battle with a brain tumor. When I was reading this passage, I had to stop several times and wipe the tears from my eyes so I could see my keyboard to continue typing.

The loss of a father—or any parent, for that matter—is a difficult and traumatic experience. Like Joseph from today's passage, this Joseph also threw himself on his father and kissed him. I'll never forget the moment when his chest stopped rising and falling during his shallow breathing. Even now as I close my eyes, I can still see it. That memory will be with me until the day I breathe my last.

Today I honor my father. Today I want you to honor a loved one that you have lost. I pray that the God of all comfort will be with you this day.

Genesis 50:7

*So Joseph went up to bury his father. All
Pharaoh's officials accompanied him*

Sometimes, as we read the Bible, we forget that the names and places are real. Because we are so far removed in time and space, we don't always connect to the characters of the story on a human level. To many people, the Bible characters are some kind of superhumans. They are not; they are real people, in a real place.

Take today's reading, for example. If we read it at face value, it simply says that all Pharaoh's officials made the journey to bury Joseph's father. Remember that Joseph was a Hebrew from a foreign land. He was an ex-con who was accused of attempted rape. Despite all this, look at the honor Joseph received at the death of his father. He wasn't treated as an alien, he was treated like one of them.

It's the same way with the family of God. It doesn't matter what your ethnic background is or what you used to do or how you used to live. When you come into the King's family, you become royalty and are treated accordingly.

Genesis 50:15

*What if Joseph holds a grudge against us and
pays us back for all the wrongs we did to him?*

It's amazing how quick Joseph's brothers were in getting
back to their old ways. No sooner had Joseph laid his
father to rest than his brothers started worrying about
what would happen to them. They thought that Joseph
was only being nice to them because of their father, Jacob.

They agreed to lie and tell Joseph that it was their
father's dying wish that Joseph forgive them for what they
did and continue to treat them well. What a sad commentary on their perception of Joseph's actions. When Joseph
wept and embraced them, couldn't they tell that it was
genuine? When Pharaoh brought them down to Egypt
and treated them like royalty because of Joseph, wasn't
that enough? Yet Joseph in his innocence assures them of
his love for them. He reminds them that they intended to
harm him, but that God meant it for good.

May we all have the attitude of Joseph when others
mistreat us.

1 Kings 2:2–3

So be strong, show yourself a man, and observe what the LORD your God requires

Today's passage focuses on the passing of the torch. Earlier we read about Jacob's last words to his sons, and today we get to listen in on King David's final words to his son Solomon, who would sit on the throne after him.

Have you ever wondered what you would say on your deathbed? I've often thought about what I want my last words to be to my wife and children. What words of wisdom or inspiration would I want to convey to them? I think it would be something along the same line as what King David told his son. He wanted to make sure his son would not only reign well as king, but that he would also live well as a human being. His encouragement was for his son to be a man by doing and observing what the Lord commanded. He was ensuring that he would see his son in eternity.

This life is but a moment; eternity is forever. May we all live our lives in such a way that we live on in eternity, and inspire those around us to do the same.

Exodus 1:8

*Then a new king, to whom Joseph meant nothing,
came to power in Egypt*

Today we begin our first devotional on the book of Exodus. The book is epic in nature and it's filled with God's promises and power.

Only a generation has passed since the death of Joseph, and we have the tragic statement found in verse 8: "Then a new king, to whom Joseph meant nothing, came to power in Egypt." It's amazing how quickly the nation of Egypt had forgotten all that Joseph had done for them.

In his paranoia, the new pharaoh treated the Israelites harshly. They were multiplying at such a rapid pace that it threatened Pharaoh. Instead of embracing this rising population, who were there as invited and honored guests of the previous pharaoh, he decided to put them to harsh labor.

I wonder if you can identify with what this generation went through. People sometimes only remember what they choose to remember. If you've been mistreated or forgotten, take heart that your God has not forgotten you.

Exodus 2:14

What I did must have become known

The stars of the majority of the book of Genesis were Abraham, Isaac, Jacob, and Joseph. And now in the book of Exodus a new face emerges—Moses. Many people learned about him from the movie *The Ten Commandments*. In that version of the film, Moses is portrayed as a confident and secure leader. The truth is, his beginnings were much more humble than that.

Moses was born into a typical Hebrew home. He was raised as royalty because of the sacrifice of his mother, who saved his life. Because of her actions, he only knew a life of privilege. One day he went out to see the people working and he saw one of his own people being beaten and treated horribly. In his anger he rose up and killed the Egyptian. The next day when he tried to stop two Hebrews from quarreling they asked if he was going to kill them too. That's when he realized that what he had done had become known.

Sometimes we act as if no one is watching, but the only One who matters is always watching.

Exodus 3:6

Moses hid his face

Afraid for his life, Moses ran into the wilderness and ended up in a village called Midian. There he decided to make a new life for himself. He got a job as a local shepherd, got married to a woman named Zipporah, and had a son with her. Basically he was trying to outrun his old life—trying to separate himself from what he had done.

What happened next must have shocked the daylights out of Moses. One day he took his father-in-law's flock of sheep to the far side of the desert to Horeb, the mountain of God. There he saw the most spectacular sight that he had seen in his life. He saw a bush that was burning, yet not being consumed by the fire. He decided to go in for a closer look, as any of us would do. Then he hears his name being called from within the bush. He doesn't know it yet, but it's the voice of Almighty God. After taking off his sandals at God's request, Moses hid his face because he was afraid to look at God.

I wonder how many of us are afraid to look at God when we come into His presence. Are we afraid to look because He's holy or because of our past?

Exodus 4:2

*Then the LORD said to him,
"What is that in your hand?"*

Although Moses wasn't a shepherd by training, he adapted to it quickly. As such, he had the same tools that any shepherd of that time period would have had. The most important item to carry was a staff. It wasn't a walking stick like many people think; it was actually a very important instrument. With the staff, the shepherd guided and led the sheep.

The staff had two main purposes. The most obvious purpose was to tap the sheep and help steer them in the right direction. Sheep have a tendency to go the wrong way, and it was the job of every shepherd to keep them on the right path. The second purpose of the staff was to guide the sheep as they crossed treacherous rivers. The shepherd would tap the larger stones in the riverbed to let the sheep know where it was safe to cross.

And so God asked Moses, "What is that in your hand?" God wasn't looking for the most educated or highest qualified person. Just like Moses, God will use us just as we are, with what we have. What do you have in your hands that you can offer to God?

Exodus 4:10

*Pardon your servant, Lord. I have never
been eloquent*

Moses is scared to death in this new calling. The very place he ran from is where God was telling him to return. And it wasn't like Moses to quietly reenter Egypt. To do what God commanded him to do, he was going to get noticed. The last time he was in Egypt, Pharaoh wanted to have him killed. Now he has to go before the present pharaoh and ask him to let the Israelites go.

We're getting ahead of ourselves...before Moses agrees to go to Egypt, he has a lengthy disagreement with God. He came up with every excuse in the book as to why he was not the right person for the job. He tried to convince God that he wasn't a good public speaker and that God's purposes would be better accomplished by sending someone else. Does this sound familiar to you?

How many times have we felt God was calling us to do something, whether great or small? What's our first response? Is it yes, Lord, I'll go? Or do we start giving God every reason why we can't do it? Know this, that if He calls you, He equips you.

Exodus 6:1

Now you will see what I will do

Moses made his debut appearance before Pharaoh. It didn't quite go the way he expected it to. Surely Pharaoh would listen to him. After all, he was sent by God. How could the mission fail? Instead of Pharaoh complying, he showed his strength by increasing the workload of the Israelites, making their already harsh working conditions more difficult.

After this failed and embarrassing meeting, the passage says that Moses returned to the Lord to speak with Him about why things had gone so badly. I can just hear Moses now, "What's the deal, God? I did what You told me to do and I failed miserably!" I'm sure we might have a very similar conversation with the Lord. I'm sure Moses was discouraged and needed to hear a comforting word from God. Then God responds and basically says, "Stick around...the show's just about to begin."

When God asks you to do something, always keep in mind who is in control. Don't worry about how it's looking at the time...He knows the beginning from the end. He's got it!

Isaiah 29:23

Stand in awe of the God of Israel

Many of the prophets wrote specifically to the people of Israel. Very few times did they concern themselves with what was going on outside their borders. Isaiah differs in that some of his prophecies are for neighboring nations as well. The striking trademark of Isaiah is his message of hope and redemption for anyone who is willing to turn back to God.

Once again Israel had fallen away from God and had chosen to follow after idols and false gods. The Lord responded harshly and threatened destruction on them. He's a jealous God and doesn't want to have second place in your life. What is beautiful here is the promise of redemption to all who will simply ask for it.

God's promise and heart for Israel is extended to you today. Even though you may have wandered away from God, the message of Isaiah is for you also. Just turn back to God. He's waiting to share His forgiveness with you. Once you receive His forgiveness, you too will stand in awe of the God of Israel.

Exodus 6:5

*Moreover, I have heard the groaning
of the Israelites*

Think of your biggest complaint. If you had the opportunity to voice your complaint to the one person who could do something about it, what would it be? This is where the Israelites were. For 430 years, they were calling out to God for deliverance. Can anyone among us even begin to imagine how frustrating and disappointing that must have been?

I wonder if they woke up every morning wondering if *that* day would be *the* day God would finally deliver them from the terrible slavery they were under. Or did they just give up and resign themselves to the fact that this was the way things were always going to be? Little did they know that their deliverance was just around the corner.

Just like God heard the cry of His people in those days, He's still listening to the cries of His people today. So often we come to God as our last resort. We seem to go to everyone else first, and then when it fails we give Him a try. Make Him first. He hears your cries and He acts on your behalf.

Exodus 7:2

You are to say everything I command you

A few days ago we first read about Moses' encounter with God at Mount Horeb. If you'll remember, he was making every excuse possible to get out of the mission God had given him. After bargaining with God, he's allowed to enlist the assistance of his brother, Aaron. Bargaining with God is foreign to those of us living today, but in biblical times, not only was it common practice and not only was it acceptable...but it seemed to work.

So now Moses and Aaron are approaching Pharaoh for a second time, since the first time around didn't go so well. I'm sure they had their own brilliant plans. They had probably worked out and rehearsed what they were going to say.

Thankfully God didn't leave it up to them and their wise words, but He instructed them and told them exactly what to say. This is something we need to learn for ourselves. Next time you go into a difficult situation and don't know what to say, pause and ask God to put His words in your mouth.

Exodus 7:12

But Aaron's staff swallowed up their staffs

Everyone loves a good show—some form of entertainment. I would have paid top dollar to have a front-row seat at the showdown between Pharaoh's magicians and Moses.

Sorcerers and magicians were commonplace in the courts of kings and pharaohs. They were called upon during times of distress or when the king needed divine guidance. I wonder if Moses and Aaron thought that what they were about to do had never been seen before. They thought everybody was about to be amazed, and that when they saw this incredible feat, surely Pharaoh would let God's people go...but the magicians had bigger snakes.

Imagine what must have been going through Moses' and Aaron's minds. There was no Plan B...this was all they had, all God had told them to do. And then they looked on with incredible surprise when Aaron's snake rose up and ate the snakes of the magicians. No matter what situation you find yourself in, trust God with what He has given you and you'll come out victorious every time.

Exodus 7:14

Then the Lord said to Moses

How many times in your life can you say that you have heard God speak to you? I mean actually hearing His voice? I don't think many people could say they have. Nine times out of ten, we hear Him in that still, small voice. You might hear His voice as you read the Bible, or you just have that sense in your heart when you pray. Moses was one of those rare characters who actually heard the voice of God.

Not just once or twice, but on a daily basis. So often you read in the Torah that God said this to Moses or God spoke to Moses, over and over again. As I was reading this week's passage it hit me—Moses spoke to God, or rather God spoke to Moses, on a regular basis. Why Moses and not you and I? It's the million-dollar question.

The truth is, not many of us can say that we have everyday, physical, two-way conversations with God. But we can speak to Him and hear from Him every day. If we spend time in prayer and reading His Word, we will hear His voice.

Exodus 9:26

The only place it did not hail was the land of Goshen, where the Israelites were

By this time in the book of Exodus, God's plan to deliver His people is in full swing. He has already sent six powerful plagues, and Pharaoh is still unwilling to let the Israelites go. Every time I read this passage I'm struck by how arrogant and stubborn he is. He would rather see his own people suffer than admit defeat.

In today's reading, the seventh plague, the plague of hail, is unleashed. Some people might think that a hailstorm isn't the worst thing in the world. The text describes this storm as the worst ever in Egypt's history. It destroyed all the livestock in the fields and was striking people down and even stripping the trees. There was complete devastation.

The amazing part is that the only place it did not hail was in the land of Goshen—where the Israelites were! What a beautiful picture of God's protection. When you are in Him, you are safe. No storm can destroy you, and no one can take you from His hand!

Exodus 9:34

He sinned again

Talk about people who never learn their lesson...or have to learn it the hard way. Some people are just stubborn. They think they can play with God and get away with it. During almost every plague, when Pharaoh couldn't take it anymore, he would summon Moses and Aaron. He would relent and say that he was ready to let the people go. Moses said that once he got out to the edge of the region he would pray for God to stop the plague. Each time this would happen, Pharaoh would change his mind and harden his heart.

In ancient times, the pharaoh was considered a god by the people. Pharaoh believed his own lies; he actually thought he was a god who could contend with the God of Israel. As we will see in future readings, he couldn't have been more wrong.

Don't be like Pharaoh. Don't just call on God when you're in trouble or when you are in a great time of need. Don't think you can outwit or outplay Him. If you repent, make sure you really mean it! If you honestly cry out to Him, He will hear and deliver you.

Ezekiel 29:13

I will gather the Egyptians

At one point in history Egypt was one of the greatest nations in the world. For many years it was the superpower of the ancient world. To this day, people marvel at the ruins of the pyramids and other mysterious buildings from the distant past.

Yet Egypt is no longer a powerful nation. Through His prophet, God had said that because of Pharaoh's actions, Egypt would never rise again to its former glory. In this passage God says that He would scatter the Egyptians all over the world and that Egypt would become a desolate wasteland for forty years. And that at the end of forty years He would bring them back from the nations. Have you ever wondered why God scattered them among the nations? I believe it was so they would know what Israel had been through and would one day go through again.

Even though Egypt sinned against God, He promised that He would one day return them to their land. That's nothing short of the great mercy of God. Many times we don't deserve His mercy, but because of His great love for us, He will always bring us back home.

Exodus 10:7

Do you not yet realize that Egypt is ruined?

Who would you say is the most stubborn and hard-headed person you know? No matter who that person is, he or she doesn't even come close to Pharaoh! This guy is thick! This is now the eighth plague, and Pharaoh still doesn't get it. He keeps allowing his people to suffer because he refuses to acknowledge God and His servant Moses.

Even his officials are starting to get impatient. The text says that at this point they are pleading with Pharaoh to let the people go. I don't think they even cared about the Israelites, they were just sick of the plagues and the massive damage it was doing on a national level. Egypt was being ruined, but Pharaoh didn't seem to care.

Too many people are like Pharaoh even today. They know they're wrong, but they won't admit it at any cost. Some people's pride has cost them their marriage, a dear friendship, and many other things. Don't be like Pharaoh and allow your pride to destroy everything you have worked so hard for. If you're wrong, admit it and move past it.

Exodus 10:21

Darkness that can be felt

What's the darkest spiritual place you have been in? Has there been an event or circumstance that has caused you to feel like you're in total darkness? You can't feel God. You can't feel your friends or family. You can't feel… period.

Imagine what it must have been like for the Egyptians during the ninth plague, total darkness. The passage says that they couldn't leave their homes; they couldn't see anyone or anything. It was total and utter darkness.

When he couldn't take it any longer, Pharaoh summoned Moses and told him that he and all the Israelites could leave, but not the livestock. Can you believe that? In a fit of rage he tells Moses to get out of his sight and never appear before him again.

Sometimes we live in darkness because we choose to live there. We go around blaming God or anyone around us, but the real person who is at fault, we don't want to blame…that's usually ourselves. Choose to live in His light! All we have to do is ask and we will receive.

Exodus 12:7, 13

*Put it on the sides and tops...the blood
will be a sign*

The final and fatal plague of the death of the firstborn was about to sweep through Egypt. Every firstborn of every kind was about to die. Yet God provided a way for His people to escape the plague. God instructed Moses to sacrifice a lamb and apply its blood to the doorpost of each home where an Israelite lived. Have you ever wondered why God gave this instruction?

Wasn't sacrificing a lamb enough? Why was the shedding of blood not enough and why put it only on the sides and the tops of the door, not on the bottom and not on the door itself? In Exodus 12:13, God said that the blood would be a sign. That God would see the blood on the door and pass over the home.

Did you know that when you apply the blood to the sides and the top of the door that it forms the letter *chet* in Hebrew, which means "life"? There was life in the blood of the lamb. When God saw the symbol of life, he passed over the home. Do you have the blood of the Lamb over the door of your heart?

Exodus 12:41

At the end of the 430 years, to the very day

Pharaoh finally broke. This time the plague struck close to home. Before this plague, only others were affected. But now that it had personally affected him, he couldn't take it anymore. He called for Moses one last time.

And just like that, it was over. The Israelites were free to go. The Egyptians were even urging them to leave. For all the Egyptians knew, more plagues would follow the longer the Israelites stayed. And literally overnight, the Israelites were no longer slaves. They gathered their people and flocks and the passage says there were about six hundred thousand men. What a day, what deliverance! God set them free after 430 years *to the day* that they entered slavery.

It was a dream come true; I'm sure the people could hardly believe it. Could it really be true, could it really be that easy? Off they went, to begin their new lives as a free people. God wants to deliver you too! Be ready. Though it may take longer than you would like, when it happens, it will happen quickly.

Exodus 12:51

And on that very day

Have you ever stopped and wondered why God set the Israelites free? Other than the obvious reason that they were slaves and were being mistreated. Throughout the Exodus story, Moses says that Pharaoh is to let the people go so that they can go celebrate a festival to the Lord.

What festival was he referring to, and why was it so important that the people celebrate it? What's being referred to here is the Passover Feast. God was instituting a means for the people to experience forgiveness. One lamb was to die for each household, and its blood would cover the sins of the people.

Once the Lord gave them the Passover instructions, He set them free. Just like that. They were like Israel's marching orders. God was also establishing a pattern that would one day be fulfilled in the Messiah.

If we observe His commands there is a promise of freedom and deliverance. We may not always understand why, but there is blessing in obedience.

Exodus 13:17

*If they face war, they might change their minds
and return to Egypt*

Do you own or have you used a GPS? I rely on mine all the time. I'm always in a new country or city where I have no idea how to drive around. I simply punch in the address of my destination and I carefully follow its directions by faith, because I have no idea how to get there myself. Many times I notice that the GPS takes me around by the longer route. I may get there a few minutes later, but at least I'll get there.

I'll bet that Moses wished he had a GPS in the wilderness. I'm sure it would have shaved a few years off the trip. Even in this passage it says that God took them the long way around. It says that it was shorter to go through Philistia, but God had a reason for doing it...so they couldn't turn back to Egypt.

So many times we wonder why God is taking us on a specific journey. We feel that there is an easier or quicker way to get something done. God isn't wasting your time; He's taking you on the route that is best and safest for you.

Jeremiah 46:28

I will discipline you but only in due measure

Today's passage is split into two separate and distinct messages. The first section deals with the partial destruction of Egypt because of how it treated Israel. The second part deals with the people of Israel and how God is going to treat them.

Much time has passed from the time of the Exodus to the days of Jeremiah. Even so, Egypt is still being punished for its mistreatment of God's chosen people. Israel is greatly loved by God, but He still disciplines them when they go off His plan.

What's remarkable about Egypt is that it is still paying for the sins of a previous pharaoh. There are consequences to one's actions. God is gracious to forgive, but the result of that sin will still bear fruit in time. Israel is told it will also be disciplined, but only in due measure. This means that God doesn't overpunish or underpunish sin. He doesn't punish us in His anger, but only according to the measure of our actions. We know that in God there is much grace, but we should also remember His justice.

Exodus 13:19

Moses took the bones of Joseph with him

The power of a promise. That's what today's passage is all about. It may not seem that way at the outset, but once you read through the entire passage it will become clear that a promise that you made, no matter how long ago, still needs to be kept.

Moses had just called down ten powerful plagues. He faced his fears of public speaking and endured ridicule from Pharaoh. And now, in the midst of a mass exodus of six hundred thousand men, he takes the time to fulfill a vow that he himself did not even make. I don't know about you, but to me that tells a lot about Moses' character.

On his deathbed Joseph asked to not be buried in Egypt. He said that one day God will come to your aid, in that day, don't forget him. Wow. That is powerful. What an example for us today.

Promises matter to God. He keeps His promises to us; in turn, we need to keep the promises that we make to others. If you can't keep it, don't make it!

Exodus 14:13

Do not be afraid. Stand firm and you will see the deliverance the Lord *will bring you today*

This by far is one of the most historic and powerful passages in the entire Bible. It's sad that so many seldom remember or read the story. The parting of the Red Sea is an epic chapter in the history of God's deliverance of His people. All Egypt had witnessed the ten plagues and had seen God's mighty hand at work. But how could He top what He had just done?

Can you imagine how afraid the people were? Moses encouraged them to stand firm because they are about to see what God will do. I have to be honest, if I were among the people, I don't know how confident I would be that we would escape with our lives. The odds weren't in their favor. It didn't look good.

That's why I love this passage. God was calling His people to trust Him in the present situation based on the evidence they had from His previous actions in their lives. When it seems darkest or most hopeless, don't despair. Look back and remember the great and mighty things God has done for you!

Exodus 14:21

Moses stretched out his hand

For me, this has to be one of the most exciting moments in all the Torah! It just doesn't get any better than this. For 430 years the Israelites were under the whips of their Egyptian taskmasters. Day after day and year after year they endured hardship, humiliation, and pain. And now, from one moment to the next, everything was about to change and things would never be the same again, for both nations.

They had the sea in front of them and Pharaoh's chariots behind them. God put a pillar of fire between them and the Egyptians so the Israelites could safely cross over to the other side. But before they could cross, Moses had to take a giant step of faith; he had to stretch out his hands over the water and believe what God had told him.

I don't know about you, but I pray I have half the faith Moses did. Imagine what we could do for God if we lived each day with that kind of faith and obedience. May God grant you this day the gift of faith to believe that through Him you are able.

Exodus 15:25

Then Moses cried out to the LORD

This is a powerful passage, yet it's funny at the same time. This is one of those passages that I was referring to earlier in this book when I said that we forget sometimes that the Bible is filled with real people and real stories. The text says they have only been traveling for three days since the Exodus, and already people are grumbling at Moses.

It's funny because they were so quick to forget all that God showed them and did for them through His servant Moses. Three days, people! That's all! Moses cries out to God. The text doesn't say, but I'm sure that the cry, in part, was out of frustration. I can't imagine how disappointed Moses was, and this was only day three of 14,400! They were complaining because there was no sweet water to drink. God showed Moses what to do, and the water turned from bitter and undrinkable to cold, refreshing, clean water.

What about you? How quick are you to turn on God or forget what He has done for you? May we never forget all that our great God has done for us!

Exodus 16:19

No one is to keep any of it until morning

Everybody knows it's not easy being a rabbi, pastor, or priest. Everyone is always counting on you and looking to you to solve their every problem. When you come through, they think you're the greatest thing since sliced bread. But if you can't give them what they want, you have a better chance of surviving a wolf pack attack. Oy vey!

Poor Moses. Now he's in the second month of the forty-year journey and the people start complaining that they have no food to eat. They actually start to reminisce about how much better their lives were in Egypt, and why had Moses taken them away from that blissful existence? I wish I were kidding, but sadly I'm not.

They said that at least in Egypt they had pots of meat and could eat all the food they wanted. So why has Moses brought them to the desert to die? Talk about drama! Despite their grumbling, God provided fresh manna for them each day. If you ever doubt God's grace, just come back and read this story again.

Exodus 17:12

Aaron and Hur held his hands up

The drama continues…first it was bitter water, then it was no food, and now it's no water. There's a pattern here that needs to be pointed out. When you get delivered from something, it's so easy to forget how terrible it was when things aren't going the way you want them to in the present. Just because there's no water, they start talking about how much water there was in Egypt. But they forgot about the lash marks on their backs. It's the classic grass-is-greener-on-the-other-side syndrome. But again, God provides water—from a rock this time.

The newly formed nation came under attack by the Amalekites. They were in no way prepared for battle. They had no training and no weapons. Surely they would be destroyed. If God had not been with them, they surely would have. But Israel had a secret weapon, stronger than anything their enemies had: they had the Lord Almighty.

Moses would raise his hands during battle. As long as he kept them up they would win, and when Moses grew tired they would start to lose when his arms would drop. Hur stepped in to help hold up Moses' arms. Whose arms has God called you to hold up?

Judges 4:7

And give him into your hands

Up to this point in the readings, it's been dominated by one gender—the males. All the great stories of Abraham, Isaac, Jacob, Joseph, and Moses—all males. This is because it was a very male-dominated society. A man's place was in the fields or at war, and the woman's place was at home with the children, caring for the home.

Today's passage is all about the heroine. The main character in the story is Deborah the judge. The Israelites are preparing for battle with Sisera, the commander of the Canaanite army. The odds are fairly even in terms of raw numbers and chariots. However, Sisera's army had been around much longer and were more than likely better trained. But under Deborah's leadership they kill every member of the army. Sisera runs away on foot to a neighboring village where he seeks refuge.

While asleep, the lady of the house drove a tent peg through his temple and killed him where he lay. Ouch! Although it was a male-dominated culture, women played important roles in carrying out God's plans. Go ladies, go!

Exodus 18:1

*Jethro... heard of everything God had done for
Moses and for his people Israel*

When you stop and think about the Exodus as it is recorded in the Torah, you don't realize it, but you're only seeing it from one perspective, that of Moses and the Israelites. But what about the rest of the world at the time? Surely the news of ten plagues and the supernatural protection of an unknown race called the Hebrews must have made the local news elsewhere?

The mighty Pharaoh was destroyed and his army was swallowed up by a parted Red Sea. The truth is that it was heard around the world. We seldom think of it, but it's true. There are extra-biblical sources that record this incredible historical event. Even Moses' father-in-law heard about what had happened to Moses and the people. I bet Jethro was pretty proud to have Moses as his son-in-law after the Exodus.

What about you? Has God done something amazing in your life? I'm sure He has. Don't keep quiet about it. Tell of His awesome power so others may know and believe that the Lord is good.

Exodus 18:18

The work is too heavy for you;
you cannot handle it alone

Some people suffer from what is called a "messiah complex." It's not an officially recognized disorder, but many have it nonetheless. They think it's their responsibility to single-handedly save the world. They either don't trust those around them or they don't believe that anyone else is capable of doing as good a job as they can.

The Israelites saw Moses as their superman. The truth is that it was wearing Moses out. He was handling all disputes and all complaints. Estimates put the Israelite population in the wilderness somewhere around one million people. Can you imagine trying to govern all those people on your own? That's what Moses was doing until his father-in-law gave him some advice. He told him that what he was doing was not good for him and not good for the people. He encouraged him to select others to help.

Let me offer you the same advice. Don't try to do everything on your own. Let others around you help. Share the burden with your brothers and sisters.

Exodus 19:4

*You yourselves have seen what I did to Egypt,
and how I carried you on eagles' wings*

The Exodus out of Egypt and the crossing of the Red Sea were historic moments for the Israelites. It was a definitive moment in time and has shaped them to this very day. Today's Israelites are the Jews, and they remember the Exodus every year during the celebration of the Passover, which we will look at in an upcoming devotional.

They knew that God was with them and that He had carried them during their forty-year journey to the Promised Land. Even in this passage God reminds the people that He carried them on eagles' wings; that without Him they would still be slaves back in Egypt.

And now another defining moment was about to take place: receiving the Ten Commandments. Not only were they the foundation for the Israelite nation, but for all of us who live today.

Let His Law be your foundation. When you feel weary and discouraged, let Him carry you.

Exodus 20:3

You shall have no other gods before me

So here it is, the moment the Israelites gathered around Mount Sinai to wait for the Lord's appearance. God said He would descend in a cloud so the people could hear Him, but they wouldn't be able to see Him. It was Moses' job to talk to Him and pass on the message to the people.

God could have started with any commandment. He could have chosen from a number of topics, but He chose this one first. Just like you would do during an important announcement or presentation, God started with what mattered most to Him. All the other commands are important, but this was the number one thing on His heart to convey to His people then and to us today.

We are to have no other gods before Him. The word "god" with a small g is anything that is worshiped or idolized. Ouch! I wonder how many of us have other gods in our lives. Our God, the only God, needs to have top priority. He must be first in our minds and hearts. Worship Him and Him alone.

Exodus 20:6

Showing love to a thousand generations

For thousands of years the Ten Commandments were the cornerstone and model for human behavior. Sadly, in recent years, there has been a move throughout the world to have any public mention of them removed. They want them out of our schools and courthouses. Why are people so against these commandments? You don't have to be Jewish or a Christian to accept that you shouldn't kill or steal.

The truth is that no one wants to be told what to do anymore. You can see it everywhere. When I was a young boy I had a healthy fear of my parents and teachers. But today, it's often the parents and teachers who have an unhealthy fear of their children and students.

God says that if we would obey His commandments, that His blessing would be on us for a thousand generations. I pray that we would uphold and honor them. That way, even though people may not be able to see them in schools or other public places, they can see them in us.

Exodus 20:8

Remember the Sabbath

I think we can agree that the Ten Commandments are universal and apply to everyone. We can also agree that if more people followed God's commandments, the world would be a much better place. Imagine a world without violence, adultery, and stealing. What a world that would be. But in the middle of the Ten Commandments, one seems to stand out: the Sabbath.

Simply put, Sabbath means rest. When God finished creating the heavens and the earth, He rested. The principle of rest was so important to God that He included it in the Ten Commandments. Why in the world would He include it there? It almost seems out of place. It's listed with adultery, murder, stealing, and others. I think I know why.

We live in such a fast-paced world. Everyone is in such a rush to get somewhere. We hardly take the time to sit back and enjoy the life that God has given us. True, it is part of the Ten Commandments, but don't look at it as having to obey. Look at it for what it is: a gift. Enjoy the opportunity to rest, to refuel, and to be renewed.

Isaiah 6:8

Here am I. Send me!

It's no wonder that Isaiah has become a favorite book of the Bible to so many people. Isaiah's prophecies are powerful and his experiences with God are inspiring. Like most prophets, he laid it all out on the line. His number one commitment was to follow and honor God and to declare His Word boldly.

His vision of the holiness of the Lord in this passage is breathtaking! He describes the angels and other heavenly creatures who are continually worshiping God and calling out His name. Even though Isaiah was only there in spirit, he still felt unworthy to be in God's presence because the Lord was so holy.

Although the heavenly creatures were worshiping God, the Lord was looking for someone that He could send and declare His message to creation. The prophet answers with "Here am I. Send me!"

I hope that's your heart today—that you would make yourself available for God to use for His Name's sake. Ask Him what He would have you do, and then do it to the best of your ability!

Exodus 21:24

Eye for eye, tooth for tooth

There are an estimated thirty-eight thousand Christian denominations in the world today. Can you believe that number? It's staggering when you stop and think of it. How can one book produce so many offshoots?

In Bible School I was taught to always read a verse in context. What does it say before and after the verse you are using? What I was never taught to do was to take the culture of the text into context. But without considering the culture, you're just asking for trouble.

Take today's passage as an example: "eye for eye and tooth for tooth." How many times have you heard this quoted when someone wants to justify an act of revenge? They always quote this Bible verse. But the fact is this verse wasn't demanding a reaction to an action, it was setting up the maximum reaction. You could only do to someone what they did to you. It was setting a limit. There are a lot more Scriptures that promote grace and forgiveness. Instead of focusing on maximum revenge, focus on maximum forgiveness. Show the same grace to others that you would have them show you.

Exodus 22:5

From the best of his own field or vineyard

Oftentimes the Torah is read without placing it within its proper cultural and geographical context. What works in one part of the world may not necessarily work in a different part of the world. I travel a lot and I can tell you that even though we are all part of the human race, we are different. Asia is not North America and the Middle East is not the Caribbean.

When the Torah is read in proper context, it takes on a much more significant tone. Look at today's passage. We have to understand that Israel was just becoming a nation. They had been slaves; they were used to being told what to do. So God had to give them laws and instructions to guide them in every avenue of daily life. The passage says that if your livestock stray into your neighbor's field or vineyard that you must pay your neighbor back with the best part of your field or vineyard. No junk, just the best.

Sometimes we have the mentality that less is best, but in God's economy, more is more! So when you bless someone, give them the best you can!

Exodus 22:21

For you were foreigners in Egypt

In Middle Eastern culture, hospitality was everything. It still is today, as it is in many parts of the world. I grew up in a Portuguese home. That meant that anyone at any time could just drop by for dinner. My mother always made enough food to feed a small army. So was the case in biblical times. Your guest came first, even when there wasn't enough food; you fed your guest first.

The Israelites were foreigners in Egypt. During the time of Joseph they were treated like family. But as time went on, they became slaves and were eventually mistreated and abused. Now God had set them free and brought them out with a mighty hand. The Israelites were traveling through the wilderness, following everywhere the pillar of fire and the cloud that led them. Eventually they would settle down and have guests who would visit them. God told them to treat visitors fairly and with respect, reminding them that they were once the foreigner.

We need to treat everyone with respect, whether they're from our culture or not. We too were once foreigners, until God brought us into His family.

Exodus 22:29

Do not hold back offerings from your granaries
or your vats

Earlier we spoke about how God was teaching the Israelites as they were learning to become a nation. For some people, the Torah is a tedious set of Bible books with little relevance for today. It's true that many of the laws contained in the Torah are not able to be kept today because society has changed and the Temple is gone. But there are morals and principles that are not only timeless but universal.

One of the principles God was instilling in the people was that of having a communal mind-set. Don't just work and think of yourself, but always have others in mind also. That's what this verse is about. God was telling the people not to stock up their shelves, so to speak, and then not give to their brother in time of need. It's so easy to focus on yourself and to forget about others. I believe that it's important to first take care of your own family, but in your excess, with your blessing, make sure to not only help others, but to teach others to do the same. Think of how much better a place the world would be if everyone looked out for each other.

Exodus 23:2

Do not follow the crowd in doing wrong

One of the most dangerous things in Israel to this day is a flash flood. They occur in the desert when there is a heavy rainstorm. The waters speed along the hard mountain surface and then fall at an alarming rate over the cliff. Anything down below is at risk of getting washed away. It can destroy roads, bridges, and even small villages.

It's amazing how quickly a small thing can become a big thing with very little effort. Think of how mobs begin. It usually starts with a few people. All it takes is for two or three to begin running, and then before you know it, everyone is running. It's very easy to get caught up in the moment.

In this passage God is warning the people not to get caught up in the mob mentality of doing wrong. Just because some people are doing something wrong doesn't mean you should do it too. Remember what your parents used to say, "If everyone jumped off a bridge, would you?" Anyone can follow the crowd and get caught up. It takes a strong person to stand up and say no, to do the right thing.

Exodus 23:20

*See, I am sending an angel ahead of you to guard
you along the way*

God promised the Israelites that as they began their journey to the Promised Land that He would be with them. That
He would guide them and protect them as they traveled.
Today's passage lays out for us some of the promises God
made to them. Here's the great thing about it: yes, those
promises were for them, but they also apply to us today.

When God sends you out on a journey, He doesn't just
pack your bag for you and then send you on your way.
No...He goes with you, to watch over you and to make
sure you're never alone. God sends an angel ahead of the
people of Israel to guard and lead them. He says that, if
they will stay on the path that's marked for them, He will
fight their battles and be an enemy to their enemies. It's
kind of like having your big brother with you when you
get into a tough situation.

God is with you. All He is asking you to do is stay on
the path He has marked out for you. How will you recognize this path? The Bible is the instruction manual. Read
it and you'll never lose your way.

Jeremiah 33:26

For I will restore their fortunes

Many people have a very fixed view of God in the Torah. I always hear people say that He is a God of judgment. That He was continually leading Israel into war and telling them to wipe out other villages and nations. True, there was a lot of war along the way. To be fair, in those days it was by war that you expanded and claimed your territory. Not like today, where we can sit down and talk rationally.

You have to read the entire Torah and the entire Old Testament to get a balanced view of who God is and how He acted. Take this passage, for instance. Israel had once again broken its covenant with God. The people had walked away from their call to be a holy nation. Instead of the anger and destruction that some people might expect, we see a loving and tender God. Even though the nations might take away Israel's wealth, God said that He would restore their fortunes.

Guess what? Even if we mess up, He's not there waiting to condemn us; rather He is waiting to restore us, to guide us back to where we need to be.

Exodus 25:2

Whose heart prompts him to give

As I travel from church to church for my speaking schedule, many times I have lunch with the pastor after the service. Once we get past the small talk and get to the meat of the conversation, almost without fail, we end up talking about finances. The pastors always ask how I do it, how I stay full time. Then they usually tell me a very familiar story of how bad things are financially in their church.

People have a problem with giving money. There, I said it, but it's true. I understand some of the reasoning behind that mentality. They've either seen or heard one too many stories about financial abuse by a church or a ministry. But I think the better explanation is that we as people don't want to part with our money.

God asked Moses to take an offering from the people to build the Tabernacle. He didn't tell him to go to the wealthy, but to go to those who felt prompted to give. We shouldn't give out of guilt or manipulation; we should give because we know it's the right thing to do and because God is the one who is prompting us to do so.

Contribution **127**

Exodus 25:15

The poles are to remain in the rings of this ark;
they are not to be removed

After months of moving from place to place, it seemed that God was finally giving the people a bit of a break. Maybe they could unpack their bags and just hang out for a while. Just because they weren't moving didn't mean they wouldn't be working. Almost immediately, God put them to work in building the holy furnishings for the Tabernacle. Today's passage focuses on the building of the Ark of the Covenant, the most important piece in the Tabernacle. Because of its importance, God gave very specific instructions, and I mean *very* specific instructions.

One of these instructions struck me as odd at first. Why did God say to make sure the carrying poles always remained in the rings, even when not in transport? This way, in time of danger or attack, they could quickly pick up the Ark and go. God wants us to be ready like that! Sometimes we're too comfortable and take so long to move when God tells us to go. If we're not ready, then the enemy can attack or we could miss God's call. Let's always be ready to move at His command.

Exodus 25:40

See that you make them according to the pattern

Yesterday we learned about how specific God was in the design and building of the furnishings for the Tabernacle. If we don't understand the reasoning behind God's thinking, the process can seem a bit overwhelming. All you have to do is read through the many chapters of the Torah that refer to the Tabernacle and you'll see how detail intense it is. The entire Tabernacle was designed to be mobile. It was a temporary dwelling place for God. It was never His plan for the people to remain in the wilderness. Everything had a purpose, and in many cases it was a shadow of things that were to come.

Too often we settle in a place where we are not supposed to be. God has a plan to get you to the Promised Land, but you have to live your life in such a way that you are ready to move at a moment's notice. Listen when God speaks; do exactly and only as He says. Everything He does in your life has a purpose, though we may not always see it at the time. It's the only way to ensure that you will get to your promised land.

Exodus 26:34

*Put the atonement cover on the ark of the
covenant law in the Most Holy Place*

Sometimes when we are reading through the book of
Exodus about all the preparations for the Tabernacle, it
can be difficult to see it in our minds. How big was it?
What did it look like when it was all done? What did
people think it was as they went by? I too had similar
questions.

During the summer of 2011, I, along with my wife and
children, had an opportunity to visit Israel's only full-
scale replica of the Tabernacle in the southern National
Park of Timna. It was amazing to get perspective. What
blew my mind was that even though it was huge, it was
portable. Sometimes they camped for a few nights and
sometimes it was for months at a time.

The Tabernacle was how God promised the people He
would dwell with them. As long as the house was in order
and they followed and obeyed all His commands, He
would dwell with them. Isn't it awesome that He no longer
needs a tabernacle, a temple, or even a church building...
but He lives in us.

Exodus 27:1

Build an altar

The latter half of the book of Exodus commits a considerable amount of text to preserving the commands and requirements that God showed Moses regarding the Tabernacle. Chapter 27 deals with the building of the altar of sacrifice.

The word "altar" gets thrown around a lot in church circles. I don't know about you, but I was brought up in a church environment where "altar calls" were commonplace. Every week the preacher would give an altar call so people could respond to his sermon. Many times it is to get right with God or to receive special prayer.

Many people went forward to lay down an addiction they were fighting or to get rid of depression or anger or many other things. But after a while I noticed that the same people were going to the altar Sunday after Sunday.

Let us not forget what the altar was for. It had one main focus: whatever you put on it would die. Is there something in your life that needs to go on the altar to die?

Exodus 27:9

Make a courtyard

During the time of the Tabernacle only the priests were allowed in the courtyard and no one was allowed to come in through the main gate. If you had a sacrifice to offer, you would bring it to the gate, where you would be met by a priest, a Levite. He would then take your sacrifice and offer it on your behalf.

Fast-forward to the time of the Temple and things had changed. Now anyone—man or woman, Jew or Gentile—was allowed to go into the outer courtyard. Once you came to the inner courtyard, the same rules applied as they did at the Tabernacle. But in Temple times, even sellers and money changers were allowed in the courtyard.

The point is that the courtyard is a place of preparation, whether you're buying or bringing your sacrifice.

God doesn't want you to remain in the courtyard. He wants you to come in through the gate, past the altar, and into His presence. He wants to have a personal relationship with you.

I Kings 6:13

*And I will live among the Israelites and will not
abandon my people Israel*

Today's passage, as chosen by the rabbis, correlates with
what we have been reading in the Torah. Moses was building the Tabernacle, and here, King Solomon is building
the First Temple. From the description that we have in
the Bible, Solomon's Temple must have been absolutely
breathtaking.

A lot of money and time was spent building it. Only the
finest wood and most skilled laborers were brought in for
the building project. Just like with the Tabernacle, God
promised Israel that He would dwell in the Temple. But
the promise to dwell with His people comes with a condition: an "if"! *If* you follow my decrees and *if* you keep my
commands...I will dwell with you. Such a small word,
but its significance cannot be minimized.

If you love God, observe His commands and statutes.
Your reward will be great. The God of heaven and earth
wants to dwell within you, the living temple.

Exodus 27:21

*Aaron and his sons are to keep the lamps burning
before the LORD*

When we hear the term "lamp" today we probably think
of a modern lamp, either run by batteries or plugged into
an electrical outlet. There was only one way to fuel your
lamp in biblical times: oil. Not the kind of oil that you
would use in a car or truck, but pure, extra-virgin olive oil.

On one of my trips to Israel I had the opportunity to
visit a couple of olive oil factories. One was in Galilee and
was very modern and full of state-of-the-art equipment.
The other one was just outside Jerusalem, and seriously,
they were using a donkey and a grinding stone like in
ancient times! Either way, only the oil that was produced
from the first crushing, which is called extra virgin, could
be used for anointing oil.

Only the first pressing could be used in the lighting of
the lamps and menorah, both in the Tabernacle and in the
Temple. Only the best was given to God. How about you?
Does God get your leftovers or does He get your very best?

Exodus 28:1

Have Aaron your brother brought to you from among the Israelites, along with his sons . . . so they may serve me as priests

When you hear the word "priest," what images are conjured up in your mind? It probably depends on your cultural and religious upbringing. A Jewish person would most likely think of a rabbi. A Catholic might think of a priest in church, with colored garments and headdress. A Christian might think of a pastor or church leader. But really, what is a priest? As defined in biblical terms, a priest could only be someone who was a direct descendant of the Aaronic bloodline, from the tribe of Levi. Today the term has been applied to those who have trained in specific religious institutions and have been so ordained.

Ultimately, a priest is someone who serves the people in God's name. They are set apart to minister to the needs of others. They are to put others before themselves. According to that definition, are we not all priests? Are we not all called to serve one another before the Lord? As His priests, we are called to be set apart, to live a life solely devoted to Him. Let us live lives that are worthy of His calling.

Exodus 28:30

Also put the Urim and the Thummim in the breastplate

There are a lot of things in the Bible that can only be understood properly within their cultural context. Then there are some things, like what is found in this passage, that we may never fully understand. I'm talking about the very secretive and highly speculative Urim and Thummim that were used exclusively by the high priest.

Many of you have heard of them before, but how many actually know what they were and what they were used for? According to the *Jewish Encyclopedia*, the Urim and Thummim were one of three methods of divine communication—the other two forms being dreams and prophets. It was through these means that the people were able to communicate with God.

Aren't you so glad today that you don't have to rely on a device or any other person in this world to talk to God, or even to hear from Him? We can go straight to Him in our time of need. Go to God, knowing that He listens. Not only does He listen, but He responds. What are you seeking Him for today?

Exodus 28:36

HOLY TO THE LORD

During the days of the Exodus, as Israel was learning to follow God, a very detailed and structured pattern of worship and tradition began to emerge. It is quite clear from the text that God had a very specific way of operating with His people. They could approach Him, but it had to be on His terms.

Objects were dedicated to the Lord and set apart for acts of worship. Common household items were anointed and blessed to be used in the Lord's service. I can remember growing up in the church, and when people would buy a new house or a car, they would ask the pastor to come over and bless it. As a young person I always found that odd. But as it turns out, it has a biblical basis.

As I read this passage I began to think about my own life. What do I have that I need to set apart and dedicate to the Lord? What about you? The truth is, all of our possessions need to be set apart for Him. Everything we have should be used as an opportunity to bless Him and an opportunity to share Him with others.

Exodus 29:18

A pleasing aroma

Not only is God's timing perfect, but it can be funny as well. As I sat down to write this evening, I just returned from my favorite coffee place here in Israel: Aroma Café. You can imagine the smile on my face as I saw today's caption, "A pleasing aroma." And then I began to think about it in the context of today's reading. Having just got off a long twelve-hour flight, the smell of freshly brewed coffee was definitely a pleasing aroma. Then I tried to look at it from God's perspective. When an animal was sacrificed on behalf of a person's sin, God says it pleases Him.

We don't have to sacrifice animals anymore for every sin we commit. Thank God! Can you imagine how many animals would have to die today? But all we have to do is approach Him in prayer. We can speak to Him directly. And when we repent of our sins and turn from our wicked ways, it's pleasing to Him.

Just like sacrifice was a pleasing aroma to Him, so is confession and forgiveness. If there is anything in your life that is out of order, offer it to Him.

Exodus 30:10

*It is most holy to the L*ORD

The concept of something or someone dying in another's place is not only pleasing to God, but according to this verse, it is holy to Him. Shedding blood for blood is the most powerful demonstration of a sacrificial gift for forgiveness.

Blood and atonement go hand in hand. I never fully understood the connection between the two. How can it be that the blood of an animal, which is a soulless creature, is able to cover my sin? And then it hit me—animals can't sin, so the blood they shed is sinless. That's why they could die on people's behalf.

So what happened to God's plan of sacrifice to cover blood when the Temple was destroyed and the sacrifices were no longer able to be carried out? How could sin be atoned for? One rabbi suggested that good works could atone for sin now.

But could an imperfect person perform enough good works to satisfy the justice of God to remove sin? It's highly unlikely. Only the Savior, only the Messiah could do such a thing.

Ezekiel 43:11

*Write these down before them so that they may
be faithful*

The prophet Ezekiel is one of my favorites, as he prophesies about the coming of the Messiah through the Eastern Gate. God then gave him a specific command to write down what he had seen so the people would not forget what had happened. If the words were not recorded, then they could not be passed down and to become part of the people's lives.

The solution is simple. Write them down—a simple but brilliant plan. Sometimes what God is saying is so beyond our comprehension that we need to write it down to be able to go back to it and read it as many times as necessary to get it to sink into our hearts and minds.

I've been writing for many years now, but I need to be more consistent with my journaling. If we write down what God is telling us as it happens, then we will have a fresh account that we can go back to anytime we need it. What has He said to you that you need to write down so you can go back, reflect on, and be encouraged?

Exodus 30:12

Each one must pay the Lord a ransom for his life

The Torah is the inspired Word of God—for me, there can be no doubt. It doesn't mean I understand everything in the Bible, or that it always makes perfect sense. Sometimes we have to dig culturally to find an application for us living today. During the Exodus Moses was commanded by God on several occasions to take a census of the people. Take a count to ensure that everyone was accounted for.

On a much smaller scale, I kind of know how Moses feels. Each time I lead a group to Israel, I'm forever counting the people, having to make sure that no one gets left behind along the way. When Moses did it, God demanded that each person pay a ransom for his or her life. If they obeyed and paid, God promised that no plague would come on them.

God said the atonement money was to be used for the service of the Temple. When you give to your place of worship, you are enabling them to carry out their mission of being a blessing to the community and greater area. May your gifts bring blessing.

When You Take **141**

Exodus 31:3

I have filled him with the Spirit of God

This is one of the coolest things I have ever read in the Torah! God was preparing the people to start building the Tabernacle. It had to be perfect. After all, it was where the presence of God was going to dwell. Before construction got underway, God first began selecting the people for various tasks.

The text says that God chose a man named Bezalel to be in charge of making artistic designs in gold, wood, and silver as well as many other crafts. What I found really cool is why God chose him. He didn't choose him because he came from a famous family or because he was wealthy or popular, but because God had filled him with His own spirit to do the various works.

Did you catch that? Bezalel was great at what he did because God is the One who designed him to have those talents. So many times we are quick to take the credit for what we are able to do. We must never forget that it is God who has blessed us with our gifts and talents, and that we need to use them in such a manner that will glorify and honor His name.

Exodus 32:1

Moses was so long in coming down from the mountain

This is one of the saddest moments in the entire Scriptures. Moses had been instructed by God to go up to the mountain. There God would give him the Ten Commandments. Talk about an incredible moment in history. While Moses is up on the mountain, the people are below and impatiently awaiting his return. The people had seen all that God had done for them. Barely any time had passed since the Exodus, and it already seemed like they had forgotten God and what He had done for them. Moses was gone a few days…to meet with God on their behalf. He wasn't away on vacation. And yet they couldn't behave while he was away?

Moses had not yet presented the commandment telling them not to worship any other gods, and the people had already melted down their gold and made it into the form of a calf. How quick are we to forget God sometimes? If He doesn't answer us right away, we turn to other gods. Be patient, be faithful; your answer is coming.

Exodus 32:14

Then the LORD relented

For those of us who live outside Israel, we can't and don't always understand God's relationship with Israel. Some people believe that God no longer has a purpose for Israel—that the Church has somehow replaced Israel. We know this can't be true because all throughout the Scriptures God reminds us of His eternal covenant. While He still loves Israel, He was constantly threatening destruction and discipline whenever their hearts wavered.

Take this passage as an example. The people had not only made a golden calf, but they were worshiping it! In His anger, God was prepared to destroy the very people He had just saved. But then something odd happened. Moses defended the people and succeeded in changing God's mind.

Moses simply reminded God of His covenant. God has made a covenant with us also! If we serve and obey Him, He promises that He will bless and keep us. Even though we deserve the punishment that our sin brings, God in His mercy is ready and willing to forgive us. We serve a great and merciful God.

Exodus 33:11

*The LORD would speak to Moses face to face, as
one speaks to a friend*

I love this verse. It's so powerful when you stop and think
about it. The text says that God would speak to Moses
face to face, as a man speaks with his friend. It's so amazing to stop and just think about that. Seeing God in nature
is one thing, but face to face? Wow! One can only imagine
how incredible that would be.

What stood out to me about this passage was the few
verses just before. It says that Moses would leave the camp
every day to go spend time with God at the Tent of Meeting. Did you catch that? The key to seeing God is spending time with Him. Not every other day, or when he
simply felt like it, but every day, no matter what.

Moses cultivated a daily relationship with God. That's
why it's so important to spend time with God daily. I'm so
glad that you're reading through the Torah on a daily
basis. When you see the face of God, you will start knowing His voice also. When you start knowing His voice,
you'll start hearing His heart.

Exodus 34:6

The compassionate and gracious God, slow to anger, abounding in love and faithfulness

Aren't you glad we serve a loving and compassionate God? I know I am. Today's passage recounts the story of how God gave the people a second chance at receiving the Law. The first time didn't go so well and ended quite badly, but God in His mercy was willing to give them another opportunity.

Moses is told to chisel out two new tablets and ascend the mountain again. God appears to Him and delivers some beautiful and comforting words. He could have destroyed the people or renounced His covenant and gone with another people. Instead He speaks words of compassion and grace. Moses asks God to stay with the people, even though they are stiff-necked.

Sometimes we act in a manner that doesn't always reflect what we say about our love for God and His Word. Even though we may fail, He is always willing to forgive and redeem us. May we too, like the Lord, be compassionate to those around us.

1 Kings 18:21

How long will you waver?

God's timing is perfect. As I write today's devotional, I just came from Mount Carmel—the very place where Elijah confronted the prophets of Baal. I was so excited as I prepared to write. With the image of the site freshly in my mind, I hope to convey to you the power of what took place on that day.

You have to remember that at Elijah's command there had been a drought for three years. Rain in that part of the world was equated with life. Without it you would die. You need it for your fields, for your animals, and for the people. Here's the great part about what Elijah did. The showdown with the prophets was with a deity they called Baal...he was the rain and fire god! So the fact that there was no rain in the first place was a proverbial slap in their faces to begin with. Then Elijah called for them to pour buckets and buckets of water on the altar. They might as well have been asked to pour out liquid gold!

Elijah proved that day beyond the shadow of any doubt that the God of Israel was the only God worth serving. We serve the almighty and awesome God.

Exodus 35:21

And everyone who was willing

Nobody likes to be told what to do. People need to be motivated by God when it comes to giving. If you try to force someone to do something, he may do it, but he will do it grudgingly. That's not how God wants you to give or live your life.

When it came time to start building the Tabernacle and forging the elements for its service, God told Moses to ask the people to give. God didn't say that He would curse or punish those who did not give, but that He wanted the gold and other elements only to be given by those who had a willing heart.

The text says that the entire community participated in the preparation of the Tabernacle instruments. Everyone contributed in the area in which they were gifted. Some could weave material while others could forge tools out of gold or silver. It didn't matter what they did; everyone's contribution was equally important.

Like the Israelites, give God what you have. Use your talents for Him. Be willing to give and serve with a willing heart. Let's build His kingdom.

Exodus 35:31

*He has filled him with the Spirit of God, with
wisdom, with understanding, with knowledge
and with all kinds of skills*

Have you ever wondered why you are the way you are?
Have you ever looked at someone who you feel is very talented or creative and asked yourself how she got that way?
The answer to those questions lies within the words of
today's reading. It's because of God and His grace.

In the time of the Bible, there were no colleges or specialized training institutions. Nobody in the camp had
graduated from college or university or had the luxury of
training in a specific trade or occupation. I've often wondered how such a seemingly primitive people could build
something so beautiful and technical.

Now we know the answer. Their gifts and talents came
from God Himself. He filled them with His spirit to
accomplish the task that was required to complete the
project. How awesome is that?

Next time you tell yourself how amazing you are,
remember the One who gave you your talent.

Exodus 36:5

The people are bringing more than enough

I absolutely love this verse. God had asked Moses to go to the people and instruct them to give an offering to build the Tabernacle. The offering wasn't in dollars but in materials necessary to build the Tabernacle. So people gave gold and silver, material for the priests' garments, and many other very important elements.

Here's the awesome part: the people gave so much that Moses had to make an announcement for the people to stop giving. They had given more than enough and there was no place to store it all. Can you imagine that happening today? Your pastor announces that you need to take up an offering to help an orphanage in a third-world country. The response to the offering is so overwhelming that the pastor has to make an announcement for the church to stop giving because there is more than enough! I pray that becomes a problem for all our congregations.

Give to God's kingdom so His love can be shared around the world.

Exodus 37:1

Bezalel made the ark

God seemed to give very specific instructions when it came to building the Ark. Two thousand years later we don't understand why God gave so many details. Why did it have to be exactly so many inches or meters in length? Why did it have to be made of one kind of wood and not another? It almost seems so arbitrary, yet the people followed these detailed instructions to the letter of the law.

The truth is that we don't always understand why God works or acts the way He does. If we can be completely honest for a moment here: sometimes it just doesn't make any sense to us. We assume there is a purpose or meaning, but we're not quite sure exactly what that is. Sometimes things happen in our lives that we just don't understand. Perhaps it's a relationship that falls apart or a loved one who becomes ill and passes away. It just seems so random and it can be incredibly frustrating and disconcerting.

While living in our lifetime we may never fully comprehend how or why God does what He does. But like the Israelites, let's learn to obey and trust.

Exodus 37:29

And the pure, fragrant incense

The Tabernacle had two main areas: the inside and the outside. That may seem a little oversimplified, but nonetheless, that's the case. This chapter deals with the many instruments inside the Tabernacle area. Each element served a specific purpose and had to be fashioned in a certain way and made with certain materials, the most detailed of which was the Ark of the Covenant. I have personally seen various replicas in Israel—one in the south of Israel at Timna National Park and a couple in Jerusalem. The detail is amazing and I can only imagine how beautiful the original was.

Other elements included the table where the daily bread offering was placed. The lampstand, or menorah as we would call it today, stood tall and had its lamps filled with oil, burning brightly day and night. The altar of incense was a key element and had a continual fragrance rising to heaven. The incense has always represented prayer.

God wants us to live a life filled with prayer. Let your prayers be like a pleasing fragrance to Him.

Exodus 38:8

From the mirrors

The element that today's passage focuses on is one of the most interesting. It's the basin for washing. It stood in the center of the courtyard and was the first thing you encountered as you entered through the gate. Before the Levites could go any further, they would have to stop here and make themselves ceremonially clean before proceeding to offer the sacrifice or light the menorah or anything else.

What most people either miss or forget is that the inside of the basin was lined with mirrors that were donated by the women. You need to remember that the purpose of the basis was to wash your sins away before you could continue to other areas of the Tabernacle. What a powerful image. As you would look into the basin to wash your hands and face, your own image would be staring you back in the face. What a great lesson. I'm sure you've heard the term, "Take a good look at yourself in the mirror."

It's so easy to judge others and point out their sins and flaws. Let's all take a good look at ourselves in the mirror before we judge others and their actions.

1 Kings 7:48

Solomon also made all the furnishings

Solomon was the son of King David, one of the most well-known figures in the entire Bible. David was known as a man who had a heart after God, despite all the sinful acts that he committed. Even though David was a great man in the eyes of the Lord, it was his son, and not him, who was charged by God to build the sacred Temple. Interesting, isn't it? David seemed like the perfect man for the job. He was greatly loved and respected by the people. He was a successful military man. He had everything in his favor, yet God did not choose him. The mandate was given to Solomon.

So many times in our lives we assume things. More often than not, that gets us in trouble or, at the very least, gets us off track. There is nothing wrong with having a vision or a dream to do something great for God. But let me ask you a question. Are you prepared to breathe the dream into existence but allow someone else to step into the limelight? If we are truly doing it for God, then it doesn't matter who gets the credit, does it? We need to be kingdom-minded in everything we say and do.

Exodus 39:43

So Moses blessed them

The verse for today comes at the end of a very long chapter that is filled with detailed commands and requirements. Some of them are so specific that it is almost impossible to imagine that the people were able to carry everything out. From this verse we learn a lot about the character of Moses. He's patient and kind. He's also a motivator.

After all the work had been done and all the orders followed, he blessed the people. He was such an encourager. Those were the exact words the people needed to hear. It would have crushed the people to hear anything short of a blessing. Receiving that blessing and approval from their leader was the icing on the cake.

Isn't that also true of us today? Doesn't every child want the approval of his parents? Doesn't he want to hear that Mom and Dad are proud? It's such a validating feeling to receive praise from someone you respect.

Use your words to be a blessing. Build people up instead of tearing them down.

Exodus 40:17

The first day of the first month

If you read the Torah carefully, a pattern begins to emerge—especially in the area of details and dates. Many times it will give you the exact year, month, and day that a significant event falls on. Many people either ignore or dismiss the dates, believing that they are no longer important or relevant.

It's also clear in the Torah that God seems to purposely cross important events with the biblical festivals. At first glance they may seem random, but upon closer observation, they can make perfect sense to us.

I'm sure many of us have had things happen to us that caused us to question God regarding the timing. Perhaps it was the loss of a job, maybe a poor medical report, or possibly even the death of a loved one. Everyone wants an answer. We want life and its issues all wrapped up in a nice little box.

If you're a person of faith, then you have to believe that all things happen, when they happen, for a reason. We need to yield everything to Him.

Exodus 40:34

The glory of the Lord filled the tabernacle

Many people look to this verse as a source of inspiration to have the divine presence of God in their midst. I've heard pastors and preachers use this text to serve as a basis for seeking or explaining a revival in their congregation. But I wonder how many of them understand the circumstances that preceded the glory of the Lord filling the Tabernacle.

Some believe that if you sing long and loud enough, that He will come. Others believe that if you pray long and loud enough, that He will come. But let's look at what it was that caused the glory of God to fill the Tabernacle. I think it will surprise a lot of people. It wasn't testimony time or a mass calling of the assembly.

The simple truth is that it was the obedience of the people that brought the glory of God. We don't have to woo God. We don't have to coax Him into bringing His presence. We don't have to whip ourselves into a frenzy. All we have to do is obey His commands and follow His instructions. In doing so, He will draw near to us and fill our hearts.

Exodus 40:37

If the cloud did not lift, they did not set out

Obedience is everything! It can make the difference between failure and success or life and death. The Israelites had to follow God's exact commands. His blessing and favor would only rest with them when they would follow His instructions. If He told them to go to battle, they would win. If they went of their own accord, they would either lose or win with heavy casualties.

The people would see the presence of God as a cloud by day and a pillar of fire by night. Wherever those two things would go, the people would follow. Sometimes the cloud would remain for several months and other times it would remain for a very short period of time. Either way, the key was obedience.

We may not have the privilege of being able to see the Lord as a cloud or a pillar of fire, but we do have His Holy Spirit within us. He dwells in us by His Spirit. He speaks to us with that still, small voice. He nudges us in our spirit to go left or right. We need to know His voice to know when to move.

1 Kings 8:2

The seventh month

If you will recall, we spoke of God's timing a few days ago. We talked about how dates are important. Many times the author doesn't tell us the background story, so we miss some of the context. The first month of the religious calendar starts with Passover, which is usually around the Gregorian calendar month of March or April. The seventh month is the holiest month on the Jewish calendar and is in late September or early October and commemorates the Day of Atonement—the holiest day of the year.

Solomon has just finished building the Temple and is now ready to transfer the Ark of the Covenant to its permanent place in the Holy of Holies in time for the Day of Atonement. Since the time of Moses, it would travel from camp to camp as God led them, but now it was time to place it where it belonged and where it would stay.

We too need to find that place where we belong. Sometimes we are all over the place. We don't stay in one place long enough to lay down roots and produce good fruit. God wants to tabernacle with us, but sometimes we have to stay put long enough for Him to work.

1 Kings 8:10

When the priests withdrew from the Holy Place

This is a very powerful story about the day Solomon brought the Ark to the Temple. Something incredible happened that day, and there is a very important lesson for us to learn in the midst of it.

It's a well-known event, and many people pray that it will happen in their place of worship. The text says that after the priests laid the Ark in the Holy of Holies, and after they withdrew from it, that the presence of the Lord filled the Temple. The presence was so strong that the priests could no longer perform their duties.

God can do whatever He wants, whenever He wants. But He also sticks to precepts that He has laid out. He asked that a place be built for Him where He could dwell with His people. He promised to live between the wings of the cherubim on the lid of the Ark. When the Ark was moved to where it belonged, that's when the power of God fell.

Find out where you belong and there God will manifest His glory!

1 Kings 8:19

You are not the one to build

Last week's passage ended with the same theme that this week's passage ends with: letting go and letting God. Remember that David was the one who had the original vision to build the Temple. More than that, he began the preparations. He ordered all the wood from Lebanon. He had all the iron he needed to manufacture the necessary amount of nails. And on and on his preparations went.

But in the end, although David was a great man, God did not allow him to be the one to build the permanent Temple. David's motives were good. As the earthly king, he lived in a large and luxurious house. "How much more does the eternal King deserve?" David thought to himself. So he set out with all his might to build his God a worthy Temple.

So you see, it's not always about what the person wants, it's about what God wants. Sometimes when things don't work out the way we want, we start to blame ourselves and throw a pity party. We start to doubt ourselves and our talents. Have you ever considered that there was nothing wrong with you—that it was not your fault—it's just that God had another plan.

Leviticus 1:1

The LORD called to Moses and spoke to him
from the Tent of Meeting

The book of Leviticus is probably the least read book of the Bible. Don't believe me? When was the last time you read it all the way through? Exactly! Some say that the Old Testament, and especially the Torah, no longer has relevance for modern-day believers. Anyone who says that has clearly not read it all the way through. The truth is that it is full of beautiful encounters between man and God. Today's verse is one of those instances. God has always desired fellowship with His creation. We see that desire in the opening verses of Genesis. Here the text says that God called to Moses and spoke to him at the Tent of Meeting.

It's great that God desired to speak with Moses, but you want to know something? He wants to speak to you too! He doesn't have favorites. He doesn't prefer to speak to one person over another.

Next time you're in your house of worship or in a time of prayer, ask Him to speak to you. He wants to! You were created by Him to have fellowship with Him.

Leviticus 2:1

It is to be of the finest flour

You may have noticed by now that sacrifices were pretty important to God. Not only during the days of the Tabernacle, but also during the Temple. It's interesting to note that God put different levels of giving requirements into the Torah. Not everyone was required to give the same amount or to give the same quality.

For those who had or made more, more was required. We see that God made giving easy; He made it achievable, from the wealthiest right down to the poorest among them. It wasn't about how much you brought to the Tabernacle, it was your heart that God was interested in.

The text says your offering is to be of the finest flour. Not of the finest flour in the world, but the finest you had. Whether you're able to give a large or a small amount in your offering, the point is that you gave.

Remember this the next time the offering plate comes by: God doesn't want your money, He wants your heart!

Leviticus 3:1

*He is to present before the L*ORD *an animal without defect*

No one really likes to get hand-me-downs. Many people have to live that way, and I completely understand. But you have to admit that there is nothing like being the first person to open an item and enjoy it. There's just something exciting about it.

I was visiting a ministry in Northern Israel that reaches out to widows and orphans, and the place was filled with hand-me-down computers that were always breaking down. It was terrible. Our ministry decided to buy them some brand-new computer equipment. They were so thankful for new and reliable equipment. If we go out of our way to bless people, even good people, with the best, should we not do the same for God? The Israelites could not bring an animal for sacrifice that had a defect. They would present the animals before the Lord to atone for their sin. It's impossible to use something tainted to remove the stain of sin.

We need to present ourselves to God in the same way, to strive to live a life that is pleasing to Him.

Leviticus 4:2

When anyone sins unintentionally and does what is forbidden

As an emerging nation, Israel was not only working on establishing its civil and legal system; its primary focus was on implementing God's laws into culture and daily life. I would encourage you to read the book of Leviticus in its entirety during the next several weeks of daily reading.

You will be amazed by the intricacies of sacrificial offerings and their requirements. God provided a way of forgiveness for every sin, but the formula for forgiveness had to be followed precisely in order to be effective.

In today's passage it seems that God had even arranged for unintentional sin to be atoned for. What an amazing thought. In their desire to obey all of the commands, in their humanity, they sometimes failed.

The same can be said of us today. We do our best to live by God's Law, but we continually fail. Perhaps there is unintentional sin in your life. Ask God to reveal it to you that you might repent.

Leviticus 5:1

He will be held responsible

As an emerging community, the people of Israel were charged by God to look out for one another. Gone were the days of "Am I my brother's keeper?" The answer to that question was an emphatic yes! The Israelites were strangers in a new territory that was filled with potentially hostile neighbors.

If people saw an injustice and chose not to do anything about it, they would be held responsible. If they didn't look out for each other, then who would? But according to the Torah, not only was it not nice to stand up and report an injustice, but you would become legally responsible for their dilemma.

How does this ancient Torah practice apply to us today? How about the next time you are driving down the road and you see a car pulled over, with smoke rising from the hood and a distressed-looking person in the car. Are you too busy to stop? Do you have somewhere more important to be? The excuses can be extensive.

As God's people, we owe it to one another to watch out for each other. Take the time . . . do what is right.

Isaiah 43:25

*I, even I, am he who blots out your
transgressions, for my own sake, and remembers
your sins no more*

Today's passage is very appropriate in the context of the timing in which I am writing this. It was during what are known in Judaism as the "High Holy Days." The three holidays that make up this sacred period are Rosh Hashanah, the Day of Atonement, and the Feast of Tabernacles. It's a season of both repentance and judgment.

During one fall season I was in Jerusalem at the Western Wall—the holiest place on earth for the Jewish people. Flocks of people were making their way down to the Western Wall to pray. I was shocked by how many people there were, and it was almost midnight. They gathered there to pray and seek forgiveness from God and to put their spiritual affairs in order.

Not everyone can go to the Western Wall in Jerusalem to pray for the forgiveness of their sins. No matter where in the world you are today as you read this: confess your sins, and He will remember them no more. What a comforting thought.

Isaiah 44:18

They know nothing, they understand nothing

One thing about the biblical prophets, they sure tell it like it is. I wonder how they would be treated by society or the religious community if they were alive today. Would we accept their messages as from God? Or would we dismiss them as spiritually unstable and continue on our way? It's an interesting thought.

In this passage the prophet is tackling the issue of idolatry, which was apparently running rampant within the community. The people had long forgotten all God had done for them to bring them out of Egypt and slavery. It is such a sad thought to consider that we are guilty of doing the same thing today. We live our lives as if we got to where we are today because of our own great abilities.

The prophets of old were constantly reminding the people to turn away from idols and turn back to God. Please let me urge you today with the same message. What the world offers you may glitter like gold, but it's only temporary. Turn to God—what He has to offer will last into eternity.

Leviticus 6:2

If anyone sins and is unfaithful to the LORD

The most important quality in any relationship is faithfulness. With that comes trust and accountability. If I trust you completely, then I trust you to be faithful. This is true of any relationship—whether it's a friendship, a business partnership, or especially in a marriage. It's also true of your relationship with God.

The most important relationship you will ever have is with the Lord. How faithful are you to Him? The difference between your relationship with those around you and your relationship with God is the fact that, even though people may disappoint you or even be unfaithful to you, He will never disappoint, abandon, or be unfaithful to you.

That's the beauty of serving God. Even though we are unfaithful sometimes, He is always true to His Word. Life can be unfair and even uncertain at times. But with the Lord, you can always have confidence in the fact that He will be there when you need Him.

Leviticus 6:13

The fire must be kept burning …
it must not go out

Every instrument in the Tabernacle served a specific purpose. Nothing was by accident but by divine design. The same can be said about your life. Have you ever had something happen that you did not plan that in the end was a great blessing to you? It was the Lord.

In the Bible there are many elements that represent various aspects of who God is. Oil is symbolic of His Holy Spirit, and often fire represents the very presence of God. We saw this during the Exodus. Remember how God led the children of Israel as a pillar of fire?

In this passage the command is to keep the fire burning at all times. This came to represent two things. First, it represented the fact that God was always with the people—that He was available whenever they needed Him. Secondly, it ensured that the altar was always ready to receive a sacrifice. That at any moment you could make atonement for your sin. That's still the case today! All you have to do is confess—at any time—and He will forgive your sins.

Leviticus 7:12

An expression of thankfulness

Everyone wants to feel appreciated. Sometimes even the smallest act of acknowledgment can make all the difference in the world. This is true even in everyday life. When you're driving and you let someone cut into your lane or make a turn, what do you look for? You look for the wave, a simple gesture of the hand.

If we show thankfulness to people around us, how much more ought we be thankful to God? You don't have to wait for the big things. You can thank Him every day for the little things that we sometimes take for granted.

Being thankful is a conscious decision. Just like being jealous or angry (or any other feeling, for that matter), you have to decide to be thankful. Can you walk? Can you see and hear? Just look around you and take the time to consider how much you have to be thankful for.

God wanted His people during the biblical period to be thankful. He wants the same of us today. Take a moment, even now, and thank Him for being alive.

Jeremiah 7:23

Walk in obedience to all I command you, that it may go well with you

How do you see God? Is He a loving creator or a judgmental deity who is looking to strike you with lightning every time you do something wrong? Did you know that the way you view God can and does greatly affect the way you choose to serve Him? If He is a loving God, then His commands are gentle and are for your own good. However, if you see Him as an angry God, then His commands are harsh and irrational.

God's words to His people should not be viewed as laws but rather, as the original language says it, instructions. Think of it in the natural sense. Each new (and often more complicated) appliance you purchase now comes with an instruction manual. The appliance may not necessarily blow up or be damaged right away. But over time, if neglected, it may break down and stop being useful.

So it is with God. His instructions are for our benefit. He's not waiting for us to disobey so He can punish us. His instructions are to help us, to bless us, and to prosper us. Follow His instruction manual.

Jeremiah 7:24

But they did not listen or pay attention

God spoke through His prophets to His people time and time again. He constantly warned the people not to stray from the path that He had laid out for them. But instead of listening to the warnings, they decided to go after their own ideas. Over and over again, the nation of Israel fell away from God and went after other gods.

God is the ultimate authority in the universe, and so He is our authority. So often we decide to go our own way. We think that our ways are better than His ways. As unbelievable as it may sound, we think we know better.

What is it about human nature that continually pushes us to seek out our own way? The Lord has clearly laid out a path for us to walk, a path that He knows is best for us, but for some reason we often feel the need to learn the hard way.

We need to understand that God always has the best intentions for us. We need to learn to trust Him, to pay attention to His direction.

Jeremiah 7:32

The Valley of Slaughter

Sometimes when we read the Bible, it's hard to picture the full story without understanding the geography of the land. Israel is a relatively small nation, yet it is massive in terms of its spiritual importance. I have had the privilege of traveling throughout Israel on a regular basis. Many times as I read the Scriptures, if I close my eyes, I can imagine myself being there.

The Valley of Slaughter that the prophet is referring to is in Jerusalem between Mount Zion and the Mount of Olives. During the Old Testament period many detestable things were done in this valley. Israel's spiritually darkest hour took place there. In this valley they offered up their children as human sacrifices to the pagan god Molek. It was an unimaginable horror.

The people thought they were doing a good thing by pleasing this pagan god. They were destroying themselves and didn't recognize that they were slaves to a phony idol. Search your heart today. Who are you trying to please, and how far are you willing to go?

Jeremiah 9:23

Let not the wise boast of their wisdom

Nobody likes a showoff. There is nothing more off-putting than a person who continually talks about himself and puts others down at the same time. It's one thing to be proud of an accomplishment, but we always have to remember to give God the glory and thanks for the talent in the first place.

In this passage, God is reminding His people to not boast in themselves. Many were going around speaking and boasting of all the money and success they had. There is nothing wrong with being successful or wealthy. The problem comes when you start to think it's because of your own greatness that you have what you have.

God said that if you are going to boast about something, boast about knowing and understanding Him. There's only one way to do that...by spending time reading His Word. So many people are trying to figure God out. If you want to know Him, He reveals Himself plainly in His Word. Read the Bible—study it, know it, and live it. Then you will have success.

Leviticus 9:22

*Then Aaron lifted his hands toward the people
and blessed them*

This passage is about the beginning of the priests' ministry and their responsibilities. You have to remember that at this point in time, the people themselves were not able to approach God. They couldn't even come into the tent. The priest did everything for the people when it came to their spiritual lives.

The priests sacrificed the animals on the people's behalf and would make atonement for their souls. There were many daily rituals and rites that could only be performed by the priests. But they were also responsible for blessing the people. They would speak God's Word and blessing over them. It's a pattern that needs to be carried out today by believers.

We are all priests. We all have the responsibility to be a blessing and to bless those around us, both in word and in deed. As people of faith, we need to be a light in a dark world. People are verbally beaten down on a daily basis. Be like Aaron: speak a blessing over and into people. Live like a priest today.

Leviticus 9:23

The glory of the Lord appeared to all the people

Everybody loves to read about the glory of the Lord appearing to people. Not just in ancient times, but still to this day. How do we get to see His glory? Is it when we whip ourselves into a spiritual frenzy during worship? Is it when we pray for hours at a time?

It's not that God can't or won't move during these times. However, we seldom think of the context in which God moved in this particular passage. It's no secret, yet very few catch it. Here it is...are you ready for it? The priests had just finished performing the sacrifices as God required; then they emerged and blessed the people. After that, that's when the text says the glory of the Lord appeared to the people. Did you catch it? The priests obeyed God's commands...and He appeared to them.

That's the not-so-secret secret to seeing God's glory. He has called us to live a life of obedience. When we walk in His ways, it brings glory to His name. And in turn, He shows us His glory. Obey Him today and release His power and glory in your life.

Eighth **177**

Leviticus 10:1

They offered unauthorized fire

Aaron's sons offered unauthorized fire to God. God struck them dead as a result of their sin. Seems a little strong, yet that is what the Scripture records. God is love and God is fair, but God is also just. We like to forget that sometimes.

Many Christians are taught that the God of the New Testament is not the God of the Old Testament—that the God of the New Testament is filled with love and compassion, and the God of the Old Testament is a violent, cruel, and angry God. That is simply not the case. The Bible says in Malachi 3:6, "I the Lord do not change."

We need to understand the holiness and justness of God. He is slow to anger and He is willing to bless and love for a thousand generations. But we have to live in the reality that there are consequences to sin.

A police officer may forgive us for running a red light, but we still have to pay the fine. We must learn to live in reverent fear before the Lord and to walk in His ways. He is a loving God who guides our steps, even when we sometimes veer off the path.

Leviticus 10:7

So they did as Moses said

Have you ever used the term "scared to death"? That would apply to today's passage. The entire camp was literally scared to death. Aaron's two sons had just been killed for offering unauthorized fire.

God spoke through Moses, and the people did as Moses said. You can be sure that no one was considering disobeying Moses after what had just happened. This wasn't the first time the people suffered death because of disobedience. Remember at Mount Sinai when they worshiped the golden calf? Three thousand were put to death that day.

People always judge the people of Israel for not "getting it." They always seemed to stray away from God, get punished, get forgiven, and then stray away again. Let's take a good long look in the mirror: are we any different today? How many times have you been forgiven for the same sin? We have all fought the same fight with our sins.

Let the fear of the Lord guide you as you strive to live for Him. He has given us His Word to be a light.

Leviticus 11:45

Therefore be holy, because I am holy

Are you holy? Am I? Is your neighbor? Can anyone truly be holy? Is there anyone you know that you can say is living a truly holy and righteous life? Consider what the Bible says in Ecclesiastes 7:20, "There is not a righteous man on earth who does what is right and never sins." Wow, no one is righteous, no one is holy! So how can we obey God's command to be holy just as He is holy? Is He setting us up for failure?

The first thing we have to do is define what "holy" actually means. In its purest definition, it simply means to be set apart. God's not asking us to live an impossible life, and then He will punish us when we fail. But we are called to be set apart, to be different from the world. God actually called His people to be a peculiar people, meaning living a different kind of lifestyle.

In this context, are you living a holy life? Do you stand out or do you just follow the crowd? It's time for us as believers to stand up for our faith and for our God. Be holy, because your God is holy.

2 Samuel 6:5

David and all Israel were celebrating

Boy did King David love to worship God! He danced before the Lord and didn't care who knew it. In this passage they have a full band playing ahead of the Ark of the Covenant. They were dancing and celebrating simply because the presence of the Lord was in their midst.

As believers, we should be the most joyous people on earth. Sadly, many times that is far from the truth. I travel a lot and speak in all kinds of different churches, from Baptist to Pentecostal and everything in between. I'm sad to report that I don't see a lot of rejoicing going on. Sometimes I have to double check the sign above the door to make sure that it's a church and not a morgue!

Nehemiah 8:10 says, "Do not grieve, for the joy of the Lord is your strength." It doesn't mean that we go around smiling and laughing all day, but it means that even in the storms of life there is an inner strength and an unspeakable lasting joy in your heart. Celebrate the fact that you are alive today and that He is in you. Let Him be your strength.

2 Samuel 6:17

*They brought the ark of the L*ORD *and*
set it in its place

After David brought the Ark to the Tent of Meeting, he set it in its proper place. Never for a moment would he even consider not placing it where it belonged. Everything was done in an order that was pleasing to God. When it came to the Lord, David seemed to almost always have his priorities in the proper place.

This is an excellent example for us. God has to be in the right place in our lives. He can't be number two, nor can He be somewhere off on the sidelines. But just like the Ark in the Tabernacle, God has to be in the center of our lives.

I know that life is busy and can be filled with all kinds of distractions. But we must never lose focus on the fact that without God we are nothing and can do nothing.

Set Him in the proper place in your life. Actively commit to keeping His Word in your heart and mind. Look for ways throughout the day to show others that He is at the center of your life.

Leviticus 12:8

If she cannot afford a lamb

Many countries offer its citizens some kind of health-care system and medical coverage. You could say this verse shows that God not only gave instructions for spiritual matters, but that He was looking after the people's physical needs as well. In this passage God is laying out the required sacrifices for purification after childbirth.

What's interesting is that God seems to have all levels of the social status covered. The standard sacrifice for childbirth was a lamb. But God made a stipulation that if you cannot afford a lamb, you can simply bring in two young doves or pigeons.

God wasn't as interested in the sacrifice itself as He was in the people's obedience. Guess what? That is still the case today. He's looking for our obedience. He's not interested in how much money you have or how famous you may or may not be. He's looking for a person whose heart is set on Him.

Take some time even now to ask yourself where God stands in your order of priority. Make changes as necessary.

Leviticus 13:45

Cry out, "Unclean! Unclean!"

Have you ever had something really embarrassing happen to you? Something so bad that you thought you would never be able to get over it and show your face in public again?

One summer, I remember driving to a church where I was going to speak that evening. I had just gone through a drive-through and got the largest coffee cup available to keep me awake for my long drive. I was wearing white pants…I had an extra-large coffee cup that spilled…can you guess what happened? Let's just say that I was very embarrassed when I arrived.

But that pales in comparison to what it must have been like for people in biblical days who were unclean for reasons that were beyond their control. Can you imagine having to yell "Unclean!" as you walked around every day so you would not contaminate those around you? This may not physically happen in the church today, but we sure do it spiritually. We're really good at isolating people who are struggling with sin. Let's love them back into the kingdom. They're feeling lonely enough.

2 Kings 4:43

They will eat and have some left

Elijah was one of the greatest prophets in Israel. He performed some incredible miracles and did amazing things for God. Then he passed his mantle on to Elisha, and it seems that a double portion was given to him. All you have to do is read through 2 Kings and you will see that the hand of God was at work in his life.

The text speaks of a dilemma faced by the prophet—too many men and not enough food. He could have panicked or he could have complained to God about his situation. He didn't do either of those things. Instead, he trusted in his God, and he had faith to believe for a miracle. This wasn't his first and it wasn't his last miracle. He lived by faith and walked in the power of God.

I don't know about you, but I would love to see those kinds of miracles in my life. But I have to be honest with myself. Do I trust God enough to see those things happen in my life? Do I panic at the first sign of trouble, or am I confident enough in who I am in God to see the miracle? The solution lies in faith, and faith comes by reading the Bible.

2 Kings 5:1

He was a valiant soldier, but he had leprosy

Racism and stereotyping is a very dangerous thing. If we buy into it, then we will begin to judge people even before we meet them. Think of some of the stereotypes that you have been raised with. What comes to your mind when I mention the following races: African American, Arab, Jewish, Native American, and so on?

I'm sorry to say that there are probably many of us who had negative images and thoughts as we read some of those races out loud. We become products of the environment that we are raised in—for better or for worse. Today's passage is about a powerful military leader whose name was Naaman. He was a valiant soldier . . . but he had leprosy.

We think that the people of the Bible period are different from us. We may be more advanced in terms of technology, but when it comes to judging people, we still have a long way to go. Don't prejudge solely based on the color of someone's skin or place of birth. Everyone deserves an equal starting ground.

2 Kings 5:3

If only my master would see the prophet who is in Samaria!

The backstory to today's passage is very important. Naaman was a military leader from Syria. He was well known for his victories, but he suffered from leprosy. It was incurable and was guaranteed to make you a social outcast as soon as it advanced to the point where you could no longer conceal it.

It's more than likely that he tried to get it treated locally without success. That's when his slave girl told him about a prophet in Samaria (Israel, that is). You see, Naaman had all the fame and success of a famous leader; yet without his health, all of it meant nothing. In 2008, my father was diagnosed with a malignant brain tumor. In that moment, I would have traded all the riches of the world to see my dad cured. In the end, he lost his life to it.

Fame and fortune seems meaningless when you don't have your health. My friends, relish the life that God has given you. Take care of this most precious gift that He has given you, and use it wisely, use it to make a difference.

2 Kings 5:11

I thought that he would surely come out to me

Have you ever met someone who thought he was better than everyone else? That the world should revolve around him? I'm sure most, if not all, of us have. Enter Naaman, great warrior and hero. He was from Syria. They were a megapower in the ancient world, well known for their military campaigns. At the head of it was our man Naaman.

A man of his social stature was used to being treated a certain way. If he were alive today, he would expect to fly first class and stay in all the five-star hotels. So when he was sent by his king with a letter to the king of Israel, I'm sure he was expecting a royal entrance. Surely they knew who he was and would treat him accordingly.

But when he arrived at the prophet Elisha's house, there was no parade or celebration. A lowly servant came to him and passed on the prophet's message. Naaman was furious. He almost missed out on a miracle because of his pride. Don't miss out on what God has for you; walk in humility and trust God.

2 Kings 5:13

*If the prophet had told you to do some great
thing, would you not have done it?*

I love this story. Today's passage picks up where we left
off yesterday. Remember how upset Naaman was that no
great prophet came out to meet him? Not only was there
no parade or big fuss, but now he was told to go dip seven
times in a filthy river. He was so upset. He was expecting
the prophet to come out and wave his hand over the
affected area and for lightning to strike and heal the blemish. Instead, he was given what he felt were a ridiculous
set of instructions.

As he was leaving, one of his servants confronted him.
This servant took a risk. As a servant you took orders and
commands—you didn't give them. He called to Naaman's
attention how foolish he was being. He was about to miss
out on his healing because it wasn't packaged the way he
wanted it to be.

Sometimes we have a fixed idea in our minds of how
God's grace should look. And if it doesn't line up with
what we imagined, we dismiss it. Don't be like Naaman . . .
come to God with an open heart.

Leviticus 14:4

And hyssop be brought for the person to be cleansed

As I travel and speak at churches regarding the symbolism of the Old Testament, I'm constantly reminding the congregation to pay attention to the details of Scripture. If you're reading a passage and something sticks out—like it's odd or it doesn't fit—then it's worth taking a closer look.

Today's passage deals with the ritual cleansing of the leper. We've had a few devotionals already dealing with this subject, but at this stage of Leviticus, we are given the exact details for the procedure of cleansing. God could have used any kind of plant as the applicator of the cleansing balm, but here He specifically lists hyssop by name. During biblical times the hyssop plant was associated with cleansing and forgiveness.

It's interesting to note that during the Exodus, God told Moses to take the blood of the lamb and apply it to the doorposts of their homes with hyssop. Thankfully, today we no longer need these complicated rituals for cleansing. We can go directly to God in prayer.

Leviticus 14:7

He is to release the live bird in the open fields

At first glance, the ritual for cleansing seems really odd. The person had to bring two birds to the priest in order to be purified. The first bird was killed and its blood was sprinkled on the second bird, which was set free. Without a proper concept of atonement, this seems like a totally absurd ritual, but this is what God was saying: there has to be an exchange of life in order for the atonement to be complete.

This whole process was for the benefit of a person who suffered from leprosy. In today's world, it's difficult for us to fathom what a person with leprosy went through in those days. We live in such a social culture. Can you imagine if you were disallowed from participating in social gatherings just because you had a blemish or a skin disease? But that's how it was in biblical times.

Why was there such a focus on removing leprosy and skin diseases? In those days it was symbolic of sin. Just like the physical disease separated you from others, so does sin separate you from God. Allow Him to purify you.

Leviticus 14:20

And they will be clean

For those of us who are believers today, it's easy to forget how difficult it was in biblical times to be forgiven. Today, all we have to do is go to Him in prayer and ask for forgiveness and we will receive it. The cleansing process was as intense as it was lonely. How thankful we should be that we no longer have to achieve forgiveness in that manner.

All of us have sinned, all of us have fallen short of what God wanted us to be. Yet He still loves and accepts us. He still lets us come into His presence. He fellowships with us and embraces us. Is that how we treat others who have sinned? Do we embrace them no matter what their past life has been? We need to remember what we were like before we found God. We were also unclean and undesirable. But He cleansed us.

Once the people followed the procedure and were declared clean, they were allowed back into the camp to live freely without limitation. Once your brothers or sisters have been forgiven, don't hold their past against them. Embrace them as God has embraced you.

Leviticus 14:36

The priest is to order the house to be emptied

When you first read this passage about how to cleanse your home of mildew, be honest, you probably wondered why God put this in the text. The Bible is a book filled with inspiration and divine direction. So what's with the steps of how to remove mildew from your home? There must be a reason for it. Rest assured, there is.

As soon as mildew was discovered, the house was to immediately be emptied so that the contents of the home would not become contaminated. The walls were inspected. Each brick was inspected. If any mildew was found, the house was to be closed for seven days and then inspected again to see if it had spread. This was done in order to save the house. You couldn't just destroy it because of a reported mildew case.

The rabbis teach that mildew is like sin. If left untreated, it can destroy a house. The parallel is striking. Now you can see why it is in the Bible. If there is any mildew (sin) in your life, get rid of it before it destroys you.

Leviticus 14:51

And sprinkle the house seven times

Today's passage is a natural progression from yesterday's reading. What should be done with the mildew-stained home after seven days? If the stain spread, then the entire house had to be destroyed. If only a few bricks were contaminated, then only those ones needed to be removed. They would be removed and taken outside the city.

However, if the mildew did not spread after the seven-day inspection period, then the house was declared to be clean, and the people could move back in. Notice again that the mixture of blood and water was applied to the house with hyssop: the plant that symbolized forgiveness.

What about people in your life, at your work or even in your family, who have had a sinful past? Do you hold it against them? Do you just discard them like an infected house? Once they have been declared clean by God, you have no right to treat them as contaminated. They have been forgiven. That means they have the full right of fellowship. Treat them as God sees them: clean!

2 Kings 7:3

They said to each other, "Why stay here
until we die?"

This is such a great story. I know it's in the Bible, and most people think the Bible is so spiritual that it actually can't have any humor in it. But that's so untrue. The Bible is filled with real people. They had the same emotions and feelings as you and I. Sometimes they were serious; sometimes they were outright hilarious.

Four lepers were outside the city gate, because in those days lepers were not allowed within the city limits. They were hungry and they were sick. They thought they were going to die of starvation. They figured they would take their chances and go into the city to find some food. Either they would die from starvation or they would die at the hands of the people. Either way, they were dead. But they took the risk, and if you read the story, it paid off big time!

Sometimes we need to have the courage of these four men. Living with regret is something that can chase you all your life. Don't let fear prevent you from obtaining what God has for you. Go for it!

2 Kings 7:19

*You will see it with your own eyes, but you will
not eat any of it!*

Believing God at His word is very important. But if we
are honest with ourselves, sometimes it can be difficult
when we are in tough circumstances. The Israelites cried
out for centuries before God answered them. I wonder if
they ever gave up hope. In this story, God gives a word
about the cost of food. Doesn't seem like a big deal. But
the penalty for not believing was death.

Remember the four lepers from yesterday's devotional?
When they entered the city they found it deserted. God
had caused the inhabitants to hear the sound of their enemy's chariots. When the lepers reported what happened
to the king, he thought it was a trap and did not go. It
turns out that no one was believing anyone that day, but
the word of the Lord did come to pass.

As punishment, the one who chose not to believe was
allowed to see the prophecy come to pass, but was not
allowed to participate in it. Sometimes we can miss out on
God's best because of doubt. Take God at His word; He
has an awesome track record.

Leviticus 16:6

Aaron is to offer the bull for his own sin

As a preacher, sometimes people forget that I, as well as other preachers, am human too—prone to the same errors in judgment as everyone else on the planet. People are shocked when they find out that I don't pray twenty-four hours a day! I wish I were kidding. They can't believe that we have hobbies and like the same things they do. Ask any pastor, priest, or rabbi and I'm sure they have had similar experiences.

During the Tabernacle days, guess what? The priests needed atonement and forgiveness too! We have to be so careful not to elevate clergy above anyone else. The only perfect One is in heaven, and He is the Creator of all things.

We live in a fallen world and are exposed to all the good and bad that it offers. The key is to keep your focus on God, not on man. People will disappoint you, but God never will! Pray for your leaders, but don't forget the One to whom we all answer.

Leviticus 16:8

*He is to cast lots for the two goats—one lot for
the LORD and the other for the scapegoat*

I don't know if you have been a believer for a few weeks or
for a few years. But at some point in your spiritual journey, you will meet people with varying degrees of opinions. Some people are okay with going to the movies while
others are not. Some people can watch certain TV shows
while others will not. We're part of a big family, and with
a big family comes diverse opinions.

The book of Leviticus is such a sacred book. In it we
are confronted over and over again with the holiness of
God. He calls us to be holy because He is holy. Yet in this
passage on national atonement, lots are used to decide
which animal lives and which one dies.

Over the years there have been so many ways to interpret biblical data. Do we allow the Scriptures to become
the measuring stick for what is right and wrong, or do our
traditions and opinions become the standard by which all
things are measured? We're family...let's give each other
some breathing space. We need to be careful to not allow
dogma or tradition to be our moral compass. The Bible,
and the Bible alone, should be that compass.

Leviticus 16:22

The goat will carry on itself all their sins

Have you ever wondered where the term "scapegoat" came from? It's actually a biblical term and comes from today's passage. The term arose from a practice instituted by God on the Day of Atonement. During the Feast of Passover a lamb is killed for each household. But during the Day of Atonement, a goat was selected to carry the sins of the entire nation.

The command from the Bible was for the high priest to lay his hands on the head of the goat. He would then symbolically transfer the sins of the people to the goat, which in turn would carry the sins of the people away into the wilderness.

This practice was modified later because sometimes the goat would come back to the place where the Tabernacle was! Imagine the horror of the people: their sins had returned to them! Eventually the goat would be taken to a high cliff and pushed off backward to ensure their sins would never return. Hence the term "scapegoat."

Leviticus 18:3

You must not do as they do in the land of
Canaan. . . . Do not follow their practices

Some religions are easily identifiable simply because of the way that people look on the outside. Judaism would definitely fall into that category. If you live in an area that has a Jewish community, then you undoubtedly have noticed that the orthodox or religious have a very particular and uniform look.

God has called the Jewish people to be a holy people: remember what holy means . . . to be set apart. They have faithfully done that for thousands of years. But it has often come at a great price. They have been hated and heavily persecuted for their obedience. Even during the biblical era they were called to be different. God told them not to be like the other nations. It would have been easier to simply blend in, but they chose to obey God rather than man.

How about us? Are we prepared to choose God over men? Are we ready to live differently, to show the world that our commitment is to God first?

Leviticus 18:21

*Do not give any of your children to be sacrificed
to Molek*

We spoke of Molek a few weeks ago and the abominable actions that people would perform in that false idol's name. It was such a wicked thing that God felt it was important to mention it again in today's text. This is something that most of us today have no way of relating to. It is unthinkable to even consider doing what they did then: they threw their children into the burning arms of a false god.

What about what we allow our children to watch or what we allow them to listen to? Do we really know who they are hanging around with and what kind of influence is affecting them? We may not have any actual idols standing in our valleys like the Israelites did, but we are far from being free of idols.

As parents and aunts and uncles and so on, we have a responsibility to our children, who are our future. The Bible says that we are to train up children in the way they *should* go, not the way they *want* to go. We all have this bent toward evil and we need to lovingly steer one another toward the right path. God's Word is a lamp unto our feet. Share His light.

Ezekiel 22:4

Have become defiled by the idols you have made

It's true that Israel is the apple of God's eye, that they are His chosen people, but they are far from perfect. Don't believe me? All you have to do is read today's passage to see what I mean.

Many times God gently woos His people back to Himself, and other times He is like a roaring lion trying to protect its cubs. Those are the actions of any loving parent. Why do we discipline our children? Because we love them. In fact, that's what God says about us. Imagine a world without discipline or rules. There would be total chaos.

Some people have a hard time seeing God as a disciplinarian; they only see Him as a loving God. Why can't He be both? There is an amazing grace to God, but there is also the side of justice and consequence. Don't mistake His mercy as weakness. Grace is a safety net, not a trampoline. Remember that He is a jealous God and He wants you all to Himself! Guard your heart and mind at all times. Live your life in a way that is pleasing to the Lord.

Ezekiel 22:19

Because you have all become dross

How would you like to be told by someone you love that you have become dull and boring and are a waste to them? It probably wouldn't feel too good. Yet that is exactly what God says to His people in today's passage. He actually calls them dross, which is a nice way to compare them to garbage. Ouch...

The nation of Israel was set apart by God to be His people. His plan was to use them to reach the nations with His message. Over time, they became complacent and grew lukewarm in their attitude toward the divine call. Through the prophet Ezekiel, God scolded the people in an attempt to wake them up from their spiritual slumber and turn their focus back to their national call.

Have we become dross in our relationship to God? Have we become religious professionals? We can talk the talk, but can we walk the walk? Ask God today to restore you to that time when He was your everything. Seek Him with all your heart, strength, and mind.

Leviticus 19:17

Do not hate your brother in your heart

Some things in this world seem like a no-brainer, but you would be amazed at how many people do it anyway. Have you ever seen people watering their lawn when it's raining? I have. You would think that people would have enough common sense, but the human mind is a peculiar thing.

Today's passage comes from a section of the Torah named "Various Laws." The entire chapter is devoted to these laws and instructions. Some are more obvious than others. It covers a wide range of topics that include obeying your parents, being honest in the workplace, and all kinds of very important character traits.

It really stood out to me that God felt it was important to include that we should not hate our brother in our hearts. This goes beyond flesh and blood. The term "brother" here is being used in its broadest sense. If we are all one big family, then how can we say we love God if we hate our brother or sister? Treat everyone around you with the same respect you would want to be treated with.

Leviticus 19:18

Do not seek revenge

They say it's easy to forgive, but not always so easy to forget. As Christians, we have a responsibility to forgive everyone and anyone who sins against us or tries to do us wrong. We are called to turn the other cheek and to love with the love of God. This is how we see this verse today. But think about this devotional for a moment. It's being written from a first-century Jewish perspective. After all, these are the same devotional readings that Jesus read. So what did this mean to Him or to someone living at the same time in the same part of the world?

Don't seek revenge against those who mean you harm. That meant that they had to forgive the Romans and other occupiers who ruled with an iron fist and who treated them like animals. Sometimes we think we have it tough, but there is always someone who has it worse.

It's not our place to seek revenge; it's our place to love regardless of whom or what the circumstances are. Leave the judging to God. After all, He said that vengeance was His anyway. It takes too much energy to hate. Loving is so much easier.

Leviticus 19:32

Stand up in the presence of the aged, show respect for the elderly

In ancient Jewish culture, the elderly were esteemed; they were people you looked up to. They were the ones whose knowledge you looked forward to receiving. The elders of the community would sit at the gates of entrance into major cities in biblical times. Those were the people that you went to when you needed counsel.

It's great to have people in your life who are your age that you can talk to and go to for advice. It can be equally rewarding to have someone in your life who has lived a full life and who has experience that you can glean from. Seniors are not to be dismissed or so easily disregarded.

It is our responsibility to instill a healthy respect in today's youth for those who are older than we are. This verse may be thousands of years old, but it's just as powerful and wise today as it was the day it was written. The seniors in our community have given so much to us, let's make sure that we give back to them.

Leviticus 19:33

*When a foreigner resides among you in your
land, do not mistreat them*

In Judaism there is something called a "mitzvoth." It literally means a commandment, but it is more generally used to refer to an act of kindness, to do a good deed. God is reminding His people here to treat the foreigner or stranger who lives among them with respect and dignity.

Remember that at one time it was the Israelites who were foreigners in Egypt. They were mistreated and taken as slaves. It was God who led them out with a mighty hand. It's easy to forget where you came from sometimes. Sadly, I see this too often in church circles. Someone finds her way into a local church, and maybe she doesn't look like she belongs, so she is given the cold shoulder and never comes back.

Church is to be a place where people can find grace and forgiveness through a personal relationship with God. Treat everyone around you fairly and lovingly. Treat them as God would. We are brothers and sisters who make up the family of God. Let love reign.

Leviticus 19:37

Keep all my decrees and all my laws and follow them. I am the LORD

Some people might read the Torah and think that it is way too strict. That God was expecting way too much from His people. Consider how lost the children of Israel would have been had it not been for the stern leading and guidance of the Lord. He put these decrees into effect for a reason. They weren't to restrict the people, they were there to protect and guide them.

They were a yoke around the people's neck. To many people, that sounds like a negative thing, but it's not. A yoke is necessary for keeping an animal on the right path so it can plow in a straight line. While in Israel, I've had the opportunity on more than one occasion to work an ancient plow with a yoked donkey. It works absolutely amazingly.

The yoke doesn't hurt the animal at all. It's just an effective way to tug it in the right direction every now and again as it starts to wander off course. God's laws are designed to protect you, not to limit you. Let Him gently nudge you in the right direction every now and then.

Leviticus 20:24

A land flowing with milk and honey

I have been to Israel dozens of times. If you haven't, then I urge you to make the trip at least once in your lifetime. Many of the Bible's sayings will come to life. The text will jump off the page. Every time I read about the land of milk and honey, I can just close my eyes and see what it means.

Did you know that the honey the Bible refers to is not the classic bees' honey that most of us are used to, but date honey? As you drive around the country, especially through the Jordan Valley, there are miles and miles of date palms. No wonder God said it would be flowing with honey. The land of Israel was their reward, not their right. Because they obeyed God's decrees, He gave them the land as a blessing.

What promised land has God given to you? I guarantee that God will do His part to get you there, but we also have to do our part. We have to obey and keep His decrees. The only thing preventing you from entering your promised land is you.

Amos 9:11

In that day I will restore David's fallen shelter

For almost two thousand years, God's people, the Jews, were exiled from their homeland of Israel. They were aliens again, living in unwelcomed lands. They had no place to go. They were mistreated everywhere they went. They were accepted at first, but as time went on, they were not only rejected, but brutally mistreated.

Racism and hatred led to evil events such as the Crusades and the Spanish Inquisition, and they culminated in the Holocaust, where six million Jews were systematically exterminated. Ezekiel's vision of the valley of dry bones had become a reality. The people lay in ruins, literally, in concentration camps.

But hear what God says in today's passage. It is so beautiful and so powerful. He said that He would restore David's fallen tent—His people. God is in the business of restoring people. He has physically restored the nation of Israel, and just like Ezekiel's vision, He wants to breathe His life into you again.

Leviticus 23:2

These are my appointed feasts

There are seven annual feasts: Passover, Unleavened Bread, Firstfruits, Pentecost, Trumpets, Day of Atonement, and Tabernacles. But what are the feasts and how or why do they apply to us as believers today? The feasts are celebrated on an annual basis. They remind us of the amazing things that God did to rescue and save His people. We can be confident that if He did it for them, then He will also do it for us today.

The word for "feast" in Hebrew is *mo'ed* and it means "an appointed time." Each of these feasts reminds us of how God has worked in humanity throughout history. They are God's way of helping us relive what He has done for us. We are to set aside the business of life and, at least annually, remind ourselves of what He has accomplished.

In this passage God says they are *His* feasts. They don't belong to the Old Testament or to a race of people. They are His to share with all people. In the next few days you will learn details about each feast and you will see how they still speak to us today.

Leviticus 23:5

The LORD's Passover

Every Christian can tell you about Good Friday and Easter, but there are very few who understand the significance of the Passover Feast. God has called us to celebrate this feast on an annual basis to remind us of all that He did for the Israelites during the Exodus. Every year for thousands of years, in each household a lamb was to be sacrificed and its blood would cover the sins of the people for yet another year.

Isn't it amazing that Jesus, who was declared to be the Lamb of God, was sacrificed on the morning of Passover? In fact, Jesus celebrated the Passover every year—first with His parents, then later with His disciples. His famous Last Supper was actually a final Passover meal. This meal is still celebrated by Jewish people all around the world today.

This book is asking, "What would Jesus read?" Others have asked, "What would Jesus do?"—He would celebrate Passover. As you celebrate it, you are remembering that He is your Lamb who was sacrificed for you. All you have to do is apply the blood to the doorpost of your heart and you will be saved.

Leviticus 23:6

You must eat bread made without yeast

During the Passover it was forbidden to eat any bread that contained yeast. At first this may sound strange. During other feasts you were allowed to eat regular bread, but why not during this one? Yeast, also known as leaven, has always been biblically associated with sin. And since the Passover is all about the lamb's blood removing sin, it stands to reason that symbolically, there should be no leaven (sin) in your life and home.

Another reason why there is no leaven during Passover is because of the speed with which God delivered them. They were enslaved for hundreds of years, and then literally overnight they were set free. They were freed so quickly that they didn't have time for their bread to rise. So from then on, there was no leaven put in the bread during Passover.

Maybe you have been praying for something for a long time and you wonder if it will ever happen. Just like the Israelites, it's coming, and when it comes, it will be quick. Don't give up, keep believing.

Leviticus 23:23

*A sacred assembly commemorated
with trumpet blasts*

As I write this devotional today, it just happens to be the evening of the Feast of Trumpets. I had not planned for it to be this way, but I guess God did. Today the Feast of Trumpets is known as Rosh Hashanah, the Jewish New Year. It also launches the holiest and most sacred time in the Jewish calendar: the Days of Awe. In Judaism it is believed that at the sound of the trumpet, or shofar, the Lord opens up His books in heaven to weigh all your good deeds against your bad ones.

Because of this, it has become known as the season of repentance—a time to get right with both man and God. In biblical times two witnesses would blow the trumpet to begin the new year. The dawning of the new moon would be the deciding factor on when it would start. It was the only feast in which no man knew the exact day or hour, only the season that it would occur.

When we hear the final trumpet sound, will we be ready? Are we living in a way that is pleasing to God? Don't get caught off guard: be ready.

Leviticus 23:26

The Day of Atonement

Without doubt, this is the holiest day on the entire Jewish calendar. The Day of Atonement is a solemn day where it is believed that God will make His judgment about the next year of your life based on how you lived the past year. Did your good deeds outweigh your bad ones? Will you have a year of blessing or cursing? Will there be life or death? All are serious questions that people grapple with during this season.

Even today, it is so solemn that the entire nation of Israel shuts down for twenty-five hours. It is a time of prayer and fasting. No cars are allowed on the roads and highways. There are no television or radio transmissions. It is a time to reflect and to inspect your heart.

Remember that the feasts were appointed or set-apart times. We can learn from this as believers. We need to set aside time every day to take a good long look at ourselves. Are we living a life that is honoring to the Lord? You may want to fast and pray during this day and ask God to show you if there is anything in your life that needs to go.

Leviticus 23:40

And rejoice before the LORD your God

The Feast of Tabernacles is the exact opposite of the Day of Atonement. It is a seven-day feast filled with great joy and celebration. It's a time to thank God for the past year—to thank Him for the harvest and the rains that brought you life.

This is also known as the Feast of Sukkot, which means "booth." It's called that because during the forty years in the wilderness the people lived in temporary booths or tents. To this day people set up booths in their yards and eat at least one meal in it, to remind them of how their ancestors had to live. The shelters also remind the people of their temporary nature. Just like life, it's only here for a season.

How religious does that sound? Not at all, right? As Christians who have been grafted into the blessings of Israel, we can share in these joyous feasts also. Celebrating them does not grant you salvation; they are to remind us of what God has done for us. Celebrate this year; tell everyone what He has done for you.

Ezekiel 44:30

So that a blessing may rest on your household

Unlike today, the priests of the Old Testament didn't have a full-time salary. They lived off the portions that the people would bring into the Tabernacle or Temple for their offerings and sacrifices.

Finances are always a touchy issue with people. Everyone knows that it takes money to run and operate a church or ministry, yet it still is a sore spot for people. The pastor can talk about God's love and all kinds of other nice subjects, but if he brings up tithing or offerings, people start getting a little fidgety in their seats. Why is that, I wonder? Could it be because we have a love affair with money? What does the Bible say in Ecclesiastes 5:10? "Whoever loves money never has money enough."

In today's passage God says that when we give to His priests we are giving to Him, and that there will be a blessing on our household. So when we give to God, we're blessing ourselves. Give with a cheerful heart so His kingdom might advance.

Leviticus 25:5

The land is to have a year of rest

When you sit down for dinner each night, do you ever wonder where it came from or how it got there? Most of us never give it a second thought. We sit down, we eat, we move on. How is it we can eat certain foods all year round, but they only naturally produce in certain seasons? Today we can manipulate the soil artificially with nutrients so farmers can produce fruit and vegetables every year...not to mention importing food.

That wasn't the case during the biblical period. They only ate what was in season. In fact, every seven years they were not allowed to plant, so that even the land would enjoy a Sabbath. That way the soil would naturally replenish itself with the appropriate nutrients. God thought of everything. What an amazing system to be put into place.

The principle of rest is found throughout the Scriptures. We live in such a busy world where business never sleeps. Between the Internet, e-mail, and everything else, we never truly have a day off. We need the Lord's Sabbath today more than ever.

Leviticus 25:18

If you want to live securely in the land, follow my decrees and obey my regulations (NLT)

What's the longest word in the English language? What's the longest word you know? For me, it was a theological term that I learned in seminary. Are you ready for it? The word is "transubstantiation." Say that one five times fast! You can Google the meaning if you like.

The point that I'm trying to make is that the power of a word is not necessarily in its size. Think of the word "no." Small word, big meaning. In the context of today's passage, I think the strongest small word is "if." *If* you obey my commands, God says, then you will live safely in the land.

Do a search throughout the Scriptures and see how many times there is a conditional promise. The word "if" appears over and over again. Such a small but powerful word. Have you ever played the "if only" game? If I hadn't gotten into the car, or if I hadn't done this or that. Don't play that game; you'll never win. What you can't control, you can't control! But today, you can decide to obey Him and to be blessed and filled with His favor.

Leviticus 25:21

I will send you such a blessing

As parents, we sometimes train our kids to act in a certain way with the promise of a blessing. It may be an ice-cream cone or a visit to their favorite toy store. The point is that blessing is a wonderful way to motivate people to do what we want. God did the same thing with the nation of Israel. We can see that here in the book of Leviticus.

He's talking about the year of jubilee, which took place every fifty years. Debts were canceled, slaves were set free, and properties were given back. It was a tremendous source of joy for the people of that time period. People worked hard to get the land to produce. Israel is a dry desert, so they relied on the natural rains to bring the harvest they needed.

The people also believed that if they followed what God had laid out for them, even if there had not been enough rain that year, that God would bless them for their obedience, and He did!

If we walk in obedience, God promises us blessing. Don't lose heart or become fearful. Trust Him.

Leviticus 25:23

*Because the land is mine and you are but aliens
and my tenants*

What do we have in this world that truly belongs to us? Think about it. How about your house or your car? Those things can be taken away from us without a moment's notice. What do we truly own? The air in our lungs right now, this moment in time, this very second. The adage is true—there are only two things that we can be sure of: death and taxes.

We can take nothing into eternity from this life. The ancient Egyptians had elaborate ceremonies and buried their dead with all their riches for the next life, only to be looted centuries later when their tombs were discovered. This land, this life, it all belongs to God. We are only His tenants on this short journey. What is a life of eighty or even ninety years in light of eternity?

How are you living today to make a difference in eternity? When it's all said and done, how will you be remembered? Do you want to be remembered for what you had, or for what you did? Start living today the way you want to be remembered.

Jeremiah 32:8

I knew that this was the word of the LORD

How great would it be to have a direct line to God! You know how in the movies, there's always that red phone on the president's desk? It's some special line to the ultimate authority. Wouldn't it be great to be able to pick up that special phone and ask God for His guidance or help?

The closest thing Israel had to that in biblical times were the prophets. They spoke to God and for God. When they opened their mouths it was as if God Himself were speaking. But what about today? Can God still speak to us, and if so, how? People say that God spoke to them about going to Bible college or to become a missionary or to marry a certain person. Then it doesn't work out...so God "tells" them something else. So how do you know when it's really Him?

There's no secret line or trick. To know God you have to spend time with Him. That's why it's so important to pray and read the Bible every day. As you do those things, you get to know His heart and nature. You'll start to recognize His voice.

Jeremiah 32:17

Nothing is too hard for you

Today's reading comes from a portion of Scripture that is in part from the prayer of the prophet. He is recounting how good God has been to him. Through prayer he is reminding himself of how God has done amazing things in his life. As I was reading this passage, I was struck by what a great idea this is.

It's so easy to forget all that God has done for us. That's why it's important to take stock of what He has done. Look back on your life, remember the difficult times that you went through and how the Lord was there. I could write pages and pages of how the Lord has helped me if I really start thinking about it.

When I went to Israel in 2002, I was lost in terms of where to go or what to do next. I had no idea that within a few months I would be on TV, traveling around the world, and authoring books.

It makes my head spin when I stop and think about it. Let me challenge you to write down what He has done, I'm sure you will be amazed at it all.

Jeremiah 32:27

*I am the Lord, the God of all mankind. Is
anything too hard for me?*

I'm so glad that the Lord has led me on this journey of
writing this daily devotional. Sometimes we tend to read
only from certain Scriptures, ones that we like or relate to
more. But having gone systematically through the Torah
and the Prophets, I have gained such a renewed respect
and awe for the written Word of God.

Don't get me wrong, I have always loved reading the
Bible. But sometimes we get stuck. Some denominations
focus on only certain parts of the Scriptures, and they
kind of ignore what doesn't line up with their theology or
point of view. But as Christians, we don't have the luxury
of picking and choosing. Either we accept and believe that
the Bible is the Word of God, or it's not. It's that simple.

Let me challenge you to do the same. Don't just rely on
my writing or anyone else's. Read the Scriptures for yourself. I think you'll come to the same conclusion that Jeremiah speaks of here: nothing is too difficult for God. Be
inspired as you read!

Leviticus 26:4

*I will send you rain in its season, and the ground
will yield its crops*

If you had to name one thing that you could not live without, what would it be? Would you say your career? Maybe your spouse or family? For some it might be something more physical, like a house or a car. What about something more basic, like food and water?

Most of us can't relate to living without food and water because we live in a land that is blessed and filled with plenty. But it's a whole other situation in Israel. It's a dry country with very little drinkable water. Its only source of clean drinking water is the Jordan River and the Sea of Galilee. It has some brutally dry winters and is often in serious need of rain. An Israeli friend of ours came to visit us in Toronto, and we took him to see Niagara Falls. It's old hat to us, but he was amazed by how much water was falling per second. If it was possible to somehow contain the amount of water that fell in one hour, Israel's water problem would be solved.

Pray for rain, both physically and spiritually in the land of Israel. Let's pray for a mighty harvest.

Leviticus 26:8

Five of you will chase a hundred

I've never been very good at math. In fact, I failed ninth-grade math twice! So as I read this passage, it was like math class all over again. Think about the numbers for a second. God said that if the people would obey His commandments and follow His decrees, five of them would chase a hundred of their enemies, and a hundred of them would chase ten thousand! Those are some pretty good odds. I would love to get ahold of an investment like that, wouldn't you? The truth is that we can—spiritually speaking, anyway.

So what in the world is God saying here? He is laying out the blessings for obedience. He couldn't make it clearer. If you obey Me, then these good things will happen for you. It's that simple.

Some people want to live a life without consequence. They want everything to work out perfectly in the end. This isn't a Hollywood movie; we're talking about real life. Live in obedience, and God says that He will help you chase your enemies; they won't be chasing you. I like those odds.

Leviticus 26:11

I will put my dwelling place among you

Think of those people in your life that you would not want to live without. Is it a spouse or a child? Perhaps a parent or a best friend? Now think about how you would feel if you could never see that person again. Could you imagine if you lost the ability to use the Internet or your cell phone? Many people would feel lost, including me. I depend on that daily contact.

That's how the Israelites felt about God. They needed Him more than anything else in this world. They had to be in constant communion with Him. They needed to know whether to turn left or right. So the very thought of being cut off from Him would have caused them to go into a panic. That's why God reassures them here in this passage.

Remaining in fellowship with God was the greatest motivation for the people of Israel. How about you? Would you be fine without talking to God or sensing His presence? Like the Israelites, we are lost without Him; He is the most important thing.

Leviticus 26:13

I broke the bars of your yoke

God is reminding His people what He did for them while they were slaves in Egypt. Time has passed and the memories of Egypt were quickly fading into the distance. So God gives them a reminder. Earlier we spoke of the purpose of the yoke, that it was designed to keep animals on the straight path while planting seeds out in the field. That's a good yoke.

Then there's the kind of yoke that you don't choose, but rather it is forced on you. That's what happened to the people in Egypt. They were forced into slavery and beaten to do the will of their Egyptian taskmasters. Think of it in this simple illustration. If you love your dog and take it for a walk, it doesn't mind being on a leash, which is a kind of yoke. But if you mistreat the animal and chain it up all day, then that's a bad yoke. That's the difference I am speaking of here.

Perhaps you are carrying a heavy yoke because of a decision you made a long time ago and you feel like it's too heavy to carry. Ask God to break the bars that are keeping you chained and live a free life.

Leviticus 26:44

*Yet in spite of this . . . I will not reject them or
abhor them*

If you have been consistently reading the Torah portions
while following this devotional schedule, then I'm sure by
now you have also noticed the very recognizable behavior
pattern of the Israelites. It's amazing to see it happen over
and over again. God establishes a covenant with them, and
the people swear to remain faithful and uphold their end
of the bargain. Two verses later the people are chasing
after false gods, God threatens to destroy or punish them,
the people repent, and God relents. This keeps happening
in cycles throughout their history as a people.

Don't be so quick to judge the Jews . . . we do it too! How
many times do people you know swear that they will
never do a certain thing again if God promises to get them
out of the situation? What do they do as soon as the coast
is clear? They go right back to their old ways. No wonder
the Bible says in Proverbs 26:11: "As a dog returns to its
vomit, so fools repeat their folly."

Let's not be fools and squander the grace of God.

Leviticus 26:45

But for their sake I will remember the covenant

Many themes begin to emerge in the Torah. You see certain patterns, both from God and from the people. The people always seemed to do the same thing over and over again. They promise to follow God and keep His statutes. And then a few verses later, they are either making their own false gods to worship or they have joined in with the locals and worshiped their false gods. And it happened over and over again.

The other pattern that emerges is that God becomes angry with the people because they have turned from His ways and have gone to other gods. Moses steps in on their behalf and convinces God not to destroy the nation. And that pattern also seems to happen time and time again.

I know it's easy to judge Israel for what they did, but let's be really honest with ourselves. How many times have we promised the Lord that from now on "it's the straight and narrow path for me," and how long before we sin again? I'm so grateful that He is slow to anger and quick to forgive. How about you?

Jeremiah 17:7

Blessed is the man who trusts in the LORD

This is one of the most awesome passages in the Bible. Each time I read it, I can feel the presence of God rising up in me. It's such a powerful verse, and it is some of the best advice you will ever get.

Jeremiah says that cursed is the man who trusts in men! That such a man won't be able to see prosperity, even if it hits him right between the eyes! Trusting in man will disappoint you every time. Men are flawed, weak, and unreliable. But blessed is the man who trusts in the Lord! That kind of a person is compared to a tree that is planted by a stream; its roots will have all the water the tree needs to survive and produce the best fruit.

Once I put down some new rolls of sod in our yard right before I had to go away for a week on a speaking trip. When I got back, the grass might as well have been hay. So I installed new grass, but this time I watered it three times a day and the roots went deep. It's so green that someone thought it was artificial turf! If you trust in God, and you're rooted in Him, you will produce fruit in season. Man may fail, but God never will!

Numbers 1:2

Take a census of the whole Israelite community

The book of Numbers starts with the numbering of all the clans of Israel. What a surprise, right? Why the constant counting of the people? Were people just wandering off and they had to keep counting them? Believe me when I say that I know how Moses feels about counting the people. Every time I lead a tour group to Israel, which I do every year, I must count the entire group at least fifty times per trip. Some people count sheep to go to sleep—I count tourists!

But seriously, why the constant counting? Remember when God promised Abraham that His descendants would be more numerous than the stars in the sky? How can you know how many people you have unless you count them? It was also a source of encouragement for the people. Each time the count got higher, that meant that God's promise to them was being fulfilled right before their eyes.

That's the great thing about God. You can track His promises in your life because they are tangible. Be encouraged today and know that God is with you.

Numbers 1:51

Anyone else who goes near it shall be put to death

I don't know how well I would have done if I had lived in Israel during the days of the book of Numbers. I'm a pretty curious person. I think it's human nature to want to push the envelope and touch or have what you're not supposed to. Just ask anyone who has ever had a toddler. As soon as you tell the child she can't touch something, that's the first thing she wants to touch when you're not looking. I think we're hardwired to be explorers.

God gave very strict commands about who could and who could not touch the Tabernacle. In fact, the only people allowed to take down or set up the Tabernacle were the Levites. You didn't even have to touch it. If you were not a Levite you couldn't even come near the Tabernacle or you would be put to death. Not a great place to be if you're an explorer like me!

There is no use in being jealous or envious of the Levites' position. Everyone had a valid function to perform. If everyone does what they are supposed to do, then it works. If not...we're in trouble.

Numbers 2:2

*The Israelites are to camp around
the Tent of Meeting*

I would love for Hollywood to make an epic film that included a scene with all the tribes of Israel gathered around the Tabernacle. Boy, that must have been an intimidating scene for anyone who was even considering an attack. Seeing that many people grouped together must have been an awesome sight to behold.

Not only is there power in numbers, there is also safety in numbers. All you have to do is track the journey of the Israelites through the desert and you will see why it is so important to travel in large numbers and to arrange yourself in such a way as to look bigger than you actually are. We see this in nature all the time. Many smaller animals have a defense system that causes them to puff up and look many more times the size than they actually are.

That's why there can be no Lone Rangers in Christianity. The enemy is always looking to attack. If you stay with the herd, you survive. If you venture out on your own, you risk being attacked. Stay with the flock and let the Shepherd watch over you.

Numbers 4:4

The care of the most holy things

The Tabernacle was an efficient and accurate atoning machine. I mean, every detail was looked after. God didn't leave anything out. From the daily sacrifices to the dimensions of the courtyard to the details of the garments and everything else, God had everything in order.

Each clan was given a different responsibility in regard to the moving of the Tabernacle. Remember that it wasn't a permanent structure. That would come later through King Solomon. This was like moving an entire community and its community center each week or so. The Kohathite clan was responsible for the holy things. That meant all of the instruments as well as the holy pieces, including the Ark and its cover. And as we have already seen, only those who were appointed to touch the holy things could do so.

In all of this, one thing becomes crystal clear: that God is a God of order. If we are made in His image, then that sense of order is also in us. We need to make sure that things in our lives are always in order.

Hosea 2:7

For then I was better off than now

There are some really beautiful and sweet prophecies in the Bible about God's relationship with Israel...but this isn't one of them. Wow, have you read the entire second chapter of Hosea? If not, read it first and then come back to this devotional so you will know what I am talking about.

God is comparing Israel to an unfaithful woman who has gone looking for her lover but can no longer find him. Like the comparison, the Israelites went after other gods, only to find out that they had abandoned them and left them with nothing. It's the classic grass-is-greener-on-the-other-side syndrome.

In the end, Israel, like the woman, came back to her husband, but only after a long and painful time. Don't be like this woman. As a believer, things aren't always peachy, they're not always perfect. But just like in any relationship, if you stick with it, you'll come through the difficult time and come back to a good place. Let God be the first one you run to, not your last resort. But just remember, if you do run, He will always be waiting for you to return.

Hosea 2:16

You will call me "My husband"; no longer call me
"My master"

Some people get hung up on titles. I see it all the time when I travel. Some pastors have to be called Pastor or Reverend. They attribute their self-worth to their title. Then you meet some other pastors who only want to be called by their first name. Don't misunderstand me, there are certain scenarios where titles must be used. I don't think it would be wise to walk into a court hearing and try to call the judge by his first name.

In ancient times, titles like "master" and "lord" were often used. Even in marriage, many times the wife would have to refer to her husband by the title "husband" and not by his name. Even Queen Esther, who was married to the king, had to use the royal title and not his name when she was in the public eye.

That's what makes this passage so precious. In a male-dominant culture, it was commonplace to call your husband "master." But here in this context, God is saying that it is no longer a one-way relationship. We love Him, and He also loves us.

Hosea 2:21

"In that day I will respond," declares the L<small>ORD</small>

Boy is it hard to forget when someone does something that is hurtful to you. I know we say with our lips that we forgive and forget, but very few people can actually forget and let the pain go. It always seems to linger in the back of our minds and it seems to have a nasty habit of rearing its ugly head when we're down.

Some people spend years in counseling while others use addictive means to dull the memories and pain. Either way, there is only one true way to get rid of the hurt, and that's by fully surrendering it to God. In this passage the Lord displays His awesome ability to forgive and forget when we sin against Him. Israel had been compared to a cheating wife who came begging back to Him. But He doesn't treat her like a cheating, begging wife. He restores her fully to where she was with Him before the act of transgression.

Oh that we would ask God to help us forgive and forget like Him! Think of how many relationships would be restored if we loved like God did.

Numbers 5:7

And must confess the sin he has committed

They say that confession is good for the soul. True. But it's also good for eternity. Unconfessed sin can and does get between you and the person you sinned against, but also between you and God. What's the best way to go about confession? Some denominations believe that all you have to do is confess your sins to a priest. Others make you confess in front of the entire congregation. The bottom line is that all we have to do is confess our sins to God and He will forgive us directly!

Did you know that in biblical times, not only were you required to confess your sin, but if it involved money you had to pay it back, plus a fifth more for compensation?

Keeping secrets is no way to live. Unconfessed sin can eat you up inside. The only way to free yourself of its venom is to confess it. Release it to God and receive His freedom today. Confessing our sins to one another releases us from the guilt and pain of that sin. But only confession to God can remove the stain of sin. Confess to Him today and be free.

Numbers 5:28

She will be cleared of guilt

It's incredible to think how much things have changed since biblical times. Our culture has come a long way. But in ancient times there was no such thing as equal rights, especially for women. In today's passage we can clearly see how much the society was dominated by men. It's stories like this that have caused much division in the Church as pertains to women's rights. Some things in the Torah are eternal and transcend time and space, like "Thou shalt not kill." But some things are culturally relevant and time specific, like the treatment of women. Already in the Second Temple period, the time of Jesus, we saw a huge leap forward in this respect. And if we fast-forward to today, we have made even more progress.

No one should be judged on the basis of gender or the color of skin. Let each person—male or female, black or white—stand or fall on his or her own individual performance. God's gift of salvation is to everyone, regardless of background. If I were preaching in a church, I'd be looking for an AMEN right about now!

Numbers 6:4

Not even the seeds or skins

Religion and rites of passage seem to go hand in hand. Throughout church history many rituals have evolved. Most of them were created in an attempt to obtain piety— that is, a higher or stronger religious sense. Christian monks moved to the Holy Land to live in caves by the Dead Sea, seeking to remove themselves from the secular world around them and to maintain ritual purity.

In the Dark Ages people would cut and chain themselves with heavy chains to atone for their sin, believing that hurting themselves would atone their souls. Even in the biblical period religious vows were taken to set one apart from others. If history teaches us anything, it's that you can't substitute true repentance and true faith with religious activity.

Samson took the Nazarene rite in today's passage. We know how things turned out for him. Just because you look religious doesn't mean that you are. And the opposite is true. Just because someone doesn't look religious, it doesn't mean that they are not. God judges the heart, not the outside.

Numbers 6:24

The LORD bless you and keep you

Without a doubt, this is one of the most beautiful blessings in the entire Scriptures. Speaking a blessing over someone was a very important part of the culture. Remember back to Abraham, Isaac, and Jacob—they would have and did do anything to receive their father's blessing. So to receive the blessing of the priest was a big deal.

Sadly, speaking a blessing over someone has not transferred well into our busy world. Nobody has time to stop. We're so busy getting to wherever it is that we have to go. That's why I'd like to recommend an ancient practice that we could adopt, even into this busy world of ours.

Every Friday night, during a ceremony known as Shabbat, Jewish fathers lay their hands on their children and speak a blessing over them. Then they turn to their wives and speak and pray a blessing on them. In a day where harsh words are spoken all the time, now more than ever we could all use a little bit more blessing. Speak life to those around you, be a blessing to someone today.

Numbers 6:25

The LORD make his face shine upon you

The book of Numbers definitely takes on a more somber tone than the previous three books of the Torah. At this point Israel has been a nation for a while. They knew they were the people of God, but they still hadn't gotten the scope of that call. They hadn't fully understood that their purpose was not only for themselves, but also for all the nations of the earth. That's a lot to take in.

They lived in dark times. Temptation was lurking around every corner. Other nations were offering them new gods to worship. They were struggling with their identity as a holy people. Does that sound familiar to anyone out there? Isn't the church struggling with the very same issues today?

We want to be holy, but at the same time, we still want to be part of the world that we left. The day is coming when we will no longer be able to keep one foot in the church and one foot in the world. That's why the words of Aaron's blessing are so powerful: in these dark times, we need the Lord to shine His face on us like never before.

Numbers 7:89

*He heard the voice speaking to him from between
the two cherubim*

Before really studying the Torah, I often wondered why
Moses was so revered by the Jewish people. I mean, I
knew he was an important guy. After all, I watched *The
Ten Commandments* movie every year on TV as a kid. But
after studying the Torah, I can see why. He was a man who
spoke to God on a daily basis, and many times, it was even
face to face.

Even Jesus quoted Moses on a regular basis. You have
to admit, that's a big deal! Even the prophecies of the
future Messiah are compared to Moses. This future Messiah will be called the second Moses. There was even a
seat in the synagogue reserved for this Messiah to sit on,
and guess what? It was called the seat of Moses. In the fall
of 2011, I was given the opportunity to sit in it, in the
ancient village of Corazim in Galilee.

I don't know about you, but I want the same relationship with God that Moses had! Do you want to hear the
voice of God speaking to you? Spend time with Him, so
that you will recognize it.

Judges 13:19

And the L<small>ORD</small> *did an amazing thing*

When I read stories like this, I wish I had been alive during Bible times. Don't you? I mean, so many amazing things happened. The beginnings of our faith were so incredible. Consider this story, the announcement of the birth of Samson.

An angel of the Lord appeared to Samson's mother and told her that she would give birth to a son, even though she was barren. Then he disappears as quickly as he had appeared. The angel appears a second time, and this time he also presents himself to Samson's father. The parents invited the angel to join them for a meal, but when they lit the flame to start cooking, the angel ascended in the flame toward heaven. Where do I start? Maybe with the fact that a barren woman conceived a child, that's a pretty cool miracle in and of itself. Or perhaps that an angel of the Lord came down from heaven and spoke with humans— that's pretty awesome too!

The Bible is an awesome book; take the time to read it every day. I guarantee your life will be changed and your faith will be strengthened.

Numbers 9:8

Wait until I find out what the LORD commands

Don't you just love to wait? I hope you can catch the sarcasm in my writing. Everybody wants everything *now*. We live in a high-speed, Wi-Fi society. I remember one time when I was traveling by car and went through a drive-through. It took them a few seconds before they took my order, and they apologized for the wait. Seriously, it was a few seconds. But that's our culture.

I wonder how we would adapt to living in the days of Moses—taking forty years to arrive at the Promised Land when it should have taken forty days. Even today's passage is about waiting. It was time for the Passover, and some people had become ceremonially unclean because of a dead body and couldn't participate. So they came to Moses looking for answers.

Instead of making a rash decision, he went to God to find out what to do. Is that your default answer—let me see what God wants me to do—or do you just do your own thing? Take the time to go to God and He will guide you.

Numbers 9:17

Whenever the cloud lifted from above the Tent,
the Israelites set out

How are you with directions? Are you directionally challenged? I used to be terrible with directions until I began traveling for a living. I'm much better at it now, but I still take my GPS with me everywhere I go. Knowing whether to turn left or right is important, but equally important is to know the traffic laws. I constantly travel outside North America and have to know the local traffic laws. Can I turn on a red light? Do I drive on the left side or the right side of the road?

Moses and the people had the best GPS in the world: they had God Himself guiding them as a cloud by day and a pillar of fire by night. They were foreigners in a strange land. They were slaves in Egypt, but at least there they knew where they were going. In the desert, they were completely lost.

But I love what the text says. They only moved when the cloud moved. That way they were in the center of God's will. Not only is that the best way to live, it's the only way to live. Listen to God's leading and move when He moves, and you will be fine.

Numbers 10:31

Please do not leave us. You know where we should camp in the desert, and you can be our eyes

On this particular journey, Moses was joined by his father-in-law. Even though Moses had the cloud of God to lead him from place to place in the wilderness, he still wanted the human eyes of his father-in-law to help find them a place to camp. That struck me as odd when I first read the passage.

It's easy for us, thousands of years later, to judge Moses. He had the presence of God leading him through the wilderness—what more did he need? Even though Moses was a great man, he was just that...a man! He was flawed like the rest of us and still had his flesh to deal with. I agree that Moses is one of the greatest biblical heroes, but at the end of the day, he's just like you and me. He enjoyed the most incredible relationship with the living God, but he still needed that human companionship, he was still human.

Like Moses, we all need people in our lives. We need friends and companions. No one wants to journey through this life alone.

Numbers 11:1

*Now the people complained about their hardships
in the hearing of the L*ORD

Just when Moses thought things were going well, the people fell back into their old ways and started to complain. God got so upset that He sent down fire to burn the edges outside the camp. It's just like in the movies when someone fires a bullet and misses the person by a few inches on purpose, just to get their attention. The people were tired of eating manna. Although it was enough to sustain them, they grew weary of eating it every day and started to dream of being back in Egypt.

They talked about all the fish they ate for free. They mentioned all kinds of fruits and vegetables that they were given to eat. I guess they forgot about the free side order of back lashing that came with every meal!

Whenever we are stuck in a rut, it's easy to look back at how things used to be. It's amazing how selective our memory can be, though. We remember the good, but not the bad. There's only one direction to move in God, and that is forward.

Numbers 11:15

If this is how you are going to treat me, put me to death right now

Poor Moses! You think it's bad to have your spouse or kids complain. Maybe as a teacher you have a class of thirty students complain. Maybe as a pastor you might have a few hundred people complain. That is still nothing compared to what Moses had to endure. He had to listen to the daily complaints of over six hundred thousand people! I think Moses reacted like any leader would in his situation. Let me paraphrase verse 15: "Kill me now!"

How would you react in his situation? He told God that he couldn't take it anymore. So God told him to bring seventy good men with him. God took some of the spirit from Moses and placed it on these men. They were given the spirit to help Moses with the daily tasks of administration. If a great leader like Moses needed help, what about us?

No man is an island unto himself. We all need to rely on somebody at some point in our lives. That's why it is so important to surround yourself with like-minded people who will be there for you when you really need them.

Numbers 12:4

Come out to the Tent of Meeting, all three of you

Talk about getting caught in the act! Aaron and Miriam thought they were talking between themselves. They got jealous because Moses was getting all the attention. So they started to grumble. The text says that the Lord heard this, referring to their gossiping and complaining. Does that freak anyone else out, or am I the only one? These two people were somewhere in the middle of the wilderness, and God heard them. Wow!

Too often we forget that God is everywhere. We do and say things in secret. The truth is that there are no secrets with God. He is everywhere all the time! So the next time you say or do something that is questionable in nature and you think that you got away with it because no one saw, think again!

God called all three of them out and forced them to confront one another and deal with the issue that was bugging them. Don't talk behind a person's back. Go to the person you have an issue with and work it out! If you don't deal with it, God will! Your choice.

Zechariah 3:4

*See, I have taken away your sin, and I will put
rich garments on you*

Zechariah is one of my favorite prophetic books of the Bible—mainly because his prophecies deal with Jerusalem. I love Jerusalem; I consider it my home away from home. It's the holy and eternal city of God. There is something so special about it. I love walking through the streets of the Old City. When I stand on the Mount of Olives and look down across the Kidron Valley and stare at the Eastern Gate, it transports me back in time.

In this passage Zechariah is given a vision from the Lord about the high priest Joshua and his garments. It's an odd vision, to be honest with you. Both Joshua and Satan are standing before the Lord. Then Zechariah notices that Joshua is dressed in filthy garments, representing the sins of the people. After Satan accuses Joshua and God defends him, he is given new robes that are clean. This represents the sin of the people being taken away.

God wants to forgive His people, but we must repent. Pray for Jerusalem today, that it may once again turn to God.

Numbers 13:2

Send some men to explore the land of Canaan

I love a good spy movie. Something about all those cool gadgets and secret missions. Joshua was about to embark on a secret spy mission. His job was to go and check out the situation in Canaan. Moses wanted to know what he was up against. What kind of people live there? What is the terrain like? And what kind of food supply could they expect?

It was a wise thing to do. It's good to know what you're walking into before you get there. That way you can make the appropriate preparations. It was the Promised Land, but they knew nothing about it except for what direction it was in. Some people like to fly by the seat of their pants. I would fall into that category. Others like to know as much as they can about a situation before they encounter it. There is wisdom in both of those camps.

After forty days of spying out the land, they came back to Moses with a report. Sometimes preparation can be your best friend when going into the unknown. Life is an adventure, but sometimes it's wise to proceed with caution. Pray before jumping.

Numbers 13:23

Two of them carried it on a pole

How big is God? How do you describe the power of an infinite being like Him? Can He be compared to the tallest building or to the highest mountain? It's a difficult concept for us to grasp. Do you stretch out your arms like a child and say, "He's this big"? Cute...but not too precise.

Once you determine the size of your God, you can begin to determine what He is able to do for you. Is He a little God that you can put in your back pocket and let Him out when you need Him? Or is He so big and so far away from you that you can't really get to Him when you need Him?

Moses had to ask himself how big his God was. He was big enough to bring ten mighty plagues and deliver them from Egypt. But was He big enough to get them to the Promised Land? The question was settled when Joshua and the others returned with a grape cluster that was so big that it took two men to carry it on a pole. Determine how big your God is today. Just remember that you serve the same God that Moses did.

Numbers 13:31

They are stronger than we are

There are two basic kinds of people in this world: optimists and pessimists. Which are you? I tend to lean toward being an optimist. Life can be tough and it can be brutal. I've always subscribed to the adage that life is serious enough. I'd rather laugh than cry.

It seems that some of the men who went out as spies leaned toward pessimism. They told Moses everything that was wrong with the land. The terrain was too tough; the people were too big...on and on the negative report went. Basically, the people there are too strong for us is what they said. But one man's voice stood out: Caleb's.

Caleb said that they should go in and take the land, that they could do it. I tend to side more with Caleb. I'd rather try something and fail than not try and never know if I could have done it. I see failure as a learning opportunity. If I didn't fail, I wouldn't learn, and I wouldn't be where I am today. Is it a risk if God is in it? Be a Caleb. If God has called you to a task, you have to believe that He will also equip you.

Numbers 14:3

Wouldn't it be better for us to go back to Egypt?

Here they go again. Defaulting back to a time when they perceived that things were better. Before you are quick to judge the Israelites about their actions, take a good long look at your own life. As humans we love our creature comforts. We enjoy stability and security. But think of all the things in this world that we would have missed out on if man had been afraid to venture out and try something new. Most good things come at great risk.

The Israelites were so serious about going back to Egypt this time that they even went as far as to say that they should select a new leader to take them back. In their grumbling, I don't think they thought the entire idea through. In their minds, their old life was waiting for them. But in reality, they would be met with cruel treatment. Because of the Israelites, Pharaoh and his entire army was killed, all the firstborns were dead, and there was lingering damage from the other nine plagues. You need to remember the situations in your past as they *really* were and not as you *thought* they were. If God is with you, then stand tall and move forward toward your promised land.

Numbers 14:11

*In spite of all the miraculous signs I have
performed among them*

Some people will never believe, no matter how much evidence is put in front of them. That's why you can't argue or debate someone into heaven. They have to experience the presence and power of God personally in their lives. But what if they experience that and they still choose not to believe? Welcome to Moses' life.

Both Caleb and Joshua stood up before the people and gave their report. They gave a moving speech about how God was with them and they would be able to take the land. Instead of riling up the crowd to go ahead, the text says that the crowd was considering stoning them. In spite of everything, the people still wanted to rebel and go back. God was prepared to destroy the people, and would have if Moses had not stepped in on their behalf.

Consider verse 18: "The LORD is slow to anger, abounding in love and forgiving sin and rebellion." Don't be like the people, who saw God's power and did not believe. Thank Him for what He has done and move forward in the victory He has given you.

Numbers 14:45

*Came down and attacked them
and beat them down*

Talk about a lose-lose situation. Because of Moses, God decided not to destroy the people, but as a punishment for their grumbling, God said that not one person who had seen their deliverance from Egypt would enter into the Promised Land. To make matters worse, the men that were sent out as spies were killed by a plague because they spread a negative report to the people and discouraged them from going up to the land. Only Caleb and Joshua were allowed to live.

When the people heard all this, they were greatly distressed and decided to repent. In their zeal they decided they would not wait for God's order to move, but they would go right away as a sign of their repentance. Moses warned them sternly not to go without God. Even though the people meant well, they should not have gone without God's go-ahead. They went and they were nearly destroyed. You see, even with the best of intentions, man's plans without God have a pattern of ending in disaster. Move forward with God, and only with God. Let Him be your only guide.

Joshua 2:10

*We have heard how the LORD dried up the water
of the Red Sea*

In today's passage the people were at the very cusp of crossing over into the Promised Land—from the mountains of Nebo across the Jordan River at Jericho. Only a few days ago, before writing today's devotional I was standing at the very spot that Scripture is referring to. It was inspiring to say the least.

Within the camp of the Israelites there were still those who had some doubts about whether or not God would be able to give them a decisive victory and the ability to claim the land that was promised to them when they left Egypt.

Yet when the spies entered Jericho, the reputation of the Lord had gone ahead of them. Rahab, whose house they entered, told them that the people of Jericho knew the city would fall at their hands because God was with them. Isn't it amazing that the very ones who see the hand of God at work are often the ones to doubt when it matters most? Don't be like that. Look back at what God has done in your life and believe.

Numbers 16:3

*They came as a group to oppose
Moses and Aaron*

Have you heard the story of Korah? I don't mean have you read it in the Scriptures. I mean, have you heard the story of Korah in your church before? Let me explain what I mean. Korah decided to lead a mutinous campaign against Moses and Aaron. He was tired of taking orders and wanted to start giving them.

He approached Moses and basically told him that he was no better than anyone else in the camp and that he had no right to stay on as leader. Korah pitched the idea that everyone was holy and that Moses had ruled long enough. Does that sound familiar at all to anyone out there?

I unfortunately have heard this many times from pastors I have visited with. If the pastor or spiritual leader isn't moving in the direction that some people think he should be going, they rise up and grumble and start trash talking—it's so sad that this still happens today. It doesn't mean that leaders are above correction, but it does mean that you should pray for your leaders and ask God how to proceed.

Numbers 16:24

Move away from the tents of Korah

As a filmmaker my imagination started running wild as I read this story again. It has all the makings of a big-screen film. Moses accepts the challenge of Korah; he doesn't shy away from it, which I find incredibly brave and bold. He tells Korah that God would be the one to choose who should rule the people and carry on as priests. The challenge was to fill their censers with incense and return to the entrance of the Tent of Meeting. Whomever God had chosen would be allowed to come near Him, the rest would die.

That's a tough challenge. But Korah didn't back down. He was so sure of himself that he and his two hundred and fifty supporters showed up and were ready to start the challenge. But before the showdown could begin, God told Moses and Aaron to step aside. The Lord had had enough of this foolishness and was ready to destroy them all.

God is patient and God is kind, but God is also God! Learn from this story. Be very careful about going against what God has ordained.

Numbers 16:31

The ground under them split apart

God is a holy God, and His power goes beyond what we can even begin to imagine. With a single word He brought the world and all that is in it into existence. His power can be terrible and furious, especially if you are on the receiving end of it.

Moses spoke to Korah and to all the people in the camp. In a matter of minutes it would become crystal clear whom God had chosen. If God had chosen Korah, then he would live a long life and die of natural causes. But if he was not chosen, then the earth would open its mouth and swallow Korah, his tents, and all his belongings. That's a pretty specific and straightforward statement. He didn't leave much room for interpretation. Do you think anyone, even for a moment, thought that such a thing could happen? But no sooner did the words come out of his mouth that what he said came to pass.

The same lesson we learned yesterday is being taught again today. It bears repeating. God is an awesome God, and you don't want to mess with Him!

Numbers 17:10

*This will put an end to their grumbling
against me*

The people had barely gotten over the shock and horror of what happened with Korah, yet God wasn't done letting the people know whom He had chosen. I don't know about you, but the whole Korah thing would have settled the issue for me. I would never challenge Moses again. But now God wanted to protect Aaron as well. He wanted to make sure that no one would challenge the priesthood.

A staff from each of the tribes was collected, and the name of the tribe was written on it. Remember that the staffs were dead, dried-up pieces of wood. All the staffs were put in front of the Ark of the Covenant in the Tabernacle overnight. Whichever staff had buds on it by morning was the tribe God had chosen to be the priests.

Not only did Aaron's staff bud, but it flowered and produced almonds as well. Talk about your slam dunks! God was ending the speculation once and for all. If God has chosen you, then He will be your testimony and no one will be able to stand against you.

Numbers 18:6

I myself have selected your fellow Levites from among the Israelites as a gift to you

It finally seems the issue of leadership has been settled in the camp. Korah is gone and Aaron's budding staff is in front of the Ark as a testimony to his calling. Now that Aaron is firmly seated as priest, God decides that now is the time to allocate helpers from the priesthood. Remember that there were more than six hundred thousand people and all of them were required to make sacrifices and atonement offerings.

There was no way that Aaron and his sons would be able to carry out all the required tasks. So God appointed the Levites as priests. Aaron and his sons were responsible to God on behalf of the people, and the Levites were responsible to the people on behalf of God.

God says that the priests were given as gifts. Have you thought of your pastor, priest, or rabbi as a gift from God to you? And if they are gifts from God, how are you treating them? They may not always be perfect, but they have been ordained by God.

Numbers 18:20

I am your share and your inheritance

If I learned anything while a pastor, it was that you don't do it for the money. There's none to be had. You do it because you are passionate about people and because you want to help them mature and develop in their faith. You can't look at being in ministry as a profession. It's a calling, and not all are called to do it. Look at what God said to Aaron in this passage. He confirmed him as priest before all the people with a mighty sign. Yet when it came to dividing up the land and allotting portions to all the tribes, Aaron was told that there would be no inheritance for him.

He was told that the Lord would be his inheritance. I know that spiritually it sounds really good, but not very practical to say the least. How would you like to tell your family that you just got the best new job, but there would be no salary or benefits? I'm not sure how well that would go over. But nonetheless, every week in churches and synagogues all over the world, men and women of God do the work that they have been called to do, with or without pay. God bless them all!

1 Samuel 12:22

The LORD will not reject his people

This week's prophetic portion builds on the fact that it is God who sets people in place—Moses and Aaron, Samuel as prophet, and now Saul as king. The title in the Bible for this passage is Samuel's farewell speech. He had served his time and had fulfilled his role as prophet. Now it was time for the rule of kings to begin.

God never intended for the people to be led by a king, but because the people saw that other nations had kings, they wanted a king. Israel again had strayed from God's purpose of making it a holy nation.

Though Israel had done many evil things—like worship the Baals and erect Ashtoreth poles—God was still committed to Israel. Although they had rejected God not just once, but many times, He said that He would still not reject His people.

He is a loving and gracious God. Even though we may turn our backs on Him, He does not turn His back on us.

Numbers 19:6

The priest is to take some cedar wood, hyssop

In today's passage we're back to some of the rituals of the Tabernacle. I must say that at first glance, many of these rituals seem odd. I'm sure I'm not the only one who has ever read this and wondered why. Why such a convoluted practice? The priest had to take a red heifer outside the camp and slaughter it. Then he would take some of the blood and sprinkle it seven times in the direction of the Tabernacle.

That was followed by some wood and hyssop, and then a ceremonial bath. What was the purpose of all of this? These were necessary steps to achieve atonement during that time. I often wonder if God made the steps so challenging on purpose, as a deterrent for people not to sin. They might think twice before sinning, knowing all they had to do to get forgiveness. As I have said many times before, we need to look for things that stand out in the passage as they may be an indication of why certain things are done. Again hyssop is used. If you remember, we talked about this being the plant of forgiveness. Aren't you thankful that we can find forgiveness by confessing directly to God?

Numbers 20:11

Water gushed out

Drama, drama, drama! My goodness! I thought the whole issue of grumbling against Moses and Aaron was taken care of with Korah and his cohorts.

The people had gathered and camped in the Desert of Zin, which is in the very south of modern-day Israel. There Miriam died and was buried. Once the people completed their mourning, it was back to business as usual, and the usual business was grumbling—this time because there was no water.

When the people first began grumbling after the Exodus, they kept saying how much better it was back in Egypt. They were singing the same song, but with slightly different lyrics. Now they were saying that they would have been better off if they had died with Korah and the others. I'm sure Moses was thinking the same thing!

God had to show the people that not only was He able to get them out of Egypt's slavery, but He was able to take them into the Promised Land. So God brought water from a rock. Not just a trickle, but gushing. When God provides…God provides!

Numbers 20:28

*Moses removed Aaron's garments and put them
on his son Eleazar*

The passing of the mantle. We read about this earlier with the prophet Elijah and his servant Elisha. In today's passage we have the passing on of the priesthood from Aaron to his son Eleazar. In the previous devotional we spoke about the time God brought forth water from the rock. What we didn't talk about was that both Aaron and Moses were told by God that they would not enter the Promised Land. So here we have the death of Aaron in the same chapter.

In biblical times, it was almost a done deal that you would take over your father's position or vocation. Eleazar would have been preparing for this moment all his life. He had some pretty big shoes to fill.

The idea of a son taking over for his father is no longer a done deal in our culture. I think of my own relationship with my son. I can't force him to wear my mantle. He has to find what God has for him. If he chooses my vocation, that's great; if it's not, that's great too. As parents, we have to pray over our kids for God's leading and direction.

Numbers 21:8

Look at it and live

At this point I'm starting to feel like a broken record, because we're back to the grumbling of the people. I might be getting tired of writing about it and you might be getting tired of reading about it, but what about poor Moses? He had to live it over and over again!

Again they complained about having no bread and water, and that they were sick and tired of manna, which they referred to as miserable food in this passage. Without hesitation, God sent poisonous snakes into their midst and the consequence of their sin resulted in the death of many of the people. The people instantly repented and God provided an antidote for them. He had Moses fashion a snake out of bronze and place it on a pole. If you had been bitten, you were to look at the bronze snake and you would live.

I wonder if this will be the last of their grumbling. If God takes the time to repeat it, then you know it is important. We need to have a grateful spirit, not a grumbling one. Let's be downright honest here…no one likes a whiner and a complainer!

Numbers 21:16

And I will give them water

I have to be honest with you, as I started to read this passage, I started getting really nervous. The people had arrived at a different place in the desert to set up camp. Every other time, they began to grumble because there was no water and started longing to go back to the land of their slavery. So I waited for the grumbling, but it never came!

Instead of grumbling, they waited for final instructions. So God took them to a place where there was a well. And where there is a well, there is water. And in the desert, where there is water, there is life. And then the most unexpected thing happens: the people break into a musical! They start singing to the Lord because they are so happy that they have water.

Still no grumbling. The passage simply says that from there they continued on their way, on their desert trek toward the Promised Land. Were the people finally getting it? That God was able to make provision for them all the way to Canaan? What a great lesson for us. Trust God. He will take care of you from the beginning right to the end.

Numbers 21:31

So Israel settled in the land of the Amorites

We need to keep in mind that the Israelites are passing through unfamiliar territory. Today we have ample maps for pretty much any part of the world. That was not the case almost four thousand years ago. They were making their own maps as they went along. Some of the locals were friendly and let them settle, while others…not so much.

This time they were to trek though the territory of the Amorites. Moses made an appeal to pass through and promised not to settle there and not to drink any of the water. They would just literally walk through without touching anything. But the king not only refused them passage, he started a war against them. He came with all his forces. But in a surprising turn of events, Israel not only defended themselves, but they actually won and got to keep the territory.

You see, when you are on the path that God has for you, there will be those who come against you. But stay the course; He will fight for you and you will win. Always walk the path that is laid out for you.

Judges 11:1

*His father was Gilead; his mother was a
prostitute*

Hi, I'm Jephthah, my mother is a prostitute!" How about
that for an introduction? This poor guy lived all his life
with that shame. He was even excommunicated, not just
socially but physically. The family unit during that time
period was of huge importance. It really did matter who
your mother and father were—what family line they were
descendants from and so on. The moment his name was
mentioned there was immediate judgment and rejection. I
found it interesting, though, that before the text tells you
who his mother was, it mentions that he was a mighty
warrior. No kidding, with a prostitute as his mother, I'm
sure he learned how to fight at a young age.

Now that time has passed, the people who had sent him
into exile were attacked and came groveling to him when
they needed a warrior. They weren't too concerned who his
mother was at that point. The point is this. You are not
responsible for who your parents were or what they did.
You can only and must only be responsible for your actions.
Live with honor and God will restore you, no matter what.

Numbers 22:18

Even if Balak gave me his palace filled with silver and gold

We are going to spend the next few days together unpacking the story of Balaam. Most people only know about Balaam's talking donkey, but there is so much more to his story—much more.

The king of Moab, whose name was Balak, was threatened by the presence of Israel on his side of the river. He had heard about what God had done for them and how they had destroyed the Amorites. So out of fear, he called for the prophet Balaam.

So, get this, Balak sends messengers to Balaam and offers to pay him a truckload of money if he will come to Moab and place a curse on the Israelites. That way, they will be weakened and Balak would be able to destroy the Israelites. So then Balaam says that he has to pray about whether or not God's will is for him to curse the Israelites. Granted, Balaam didn't know they were God's chosen people at that time. But take my advice—if someone offers you money to curse someone, you don't have to pray about it. The answer is a resounding no!

Numbers 22:31

Then the Lord opened Balaam's eyes

Early in the morning, Balaam set out on his journey to Moab to find out if it was God's will for him to curse the Israelites. The text says that God was very angry with Balaam and sent an angel to block the road. The donkey saw the angel and veered into a field. So Balaam beat the donkey until he went back on the road.

The angel appeared a second time and again it spooked the donkey, this time crushing Balaam's foot, so he beat the donkey a second time. Finally, the angel stood in the way so the donkey could not go around, so it just lay down. Again Balaam beat the donkey with his staff. At this, the Lord opened the donkey's mouth and it spoke! Can you imagine the shock that Balaam received?

The donkey starts an intelligent conversation, not just a few words. After a few moments God opened up Balaam's eyes to see what his donkey saw, then he understood. Sometimes we judge situations without knowing the background. Maybe we all need to pray and ask God to open our eyes.

Numbers 23:11

But you have done nothing but bless them

Balak, the king of Moab, was furious that the prophet didn't come to him right away. When Balaam finally arrived, they got straight to business. Balak offered sacrifices, and Balaam told him to build seven altars while he went to seek God for direction. After meeting with God, Balaam went back with a message that he knew would be displeasing to the king. But he had to say what God had said, not what the king wanted to hear.

Sometimes we do the same thing Balak does; we just won't admit it, though. We want an answer from God, or we say we do, but we're actually just wanting to have our own ideas confirmed.

The prophet came back and said that he could not curse what God had not cursed, nor could he speak a single negative word against God's chosen people. You can imagine how furious the king was now. Balak said that he brought the prophet to curse his enemies, but all he had done was bless his enemies. I'll say it again, you can't pray for your will to be done; you have to seek out God's will.

Numbers 23:19

Does He promise and not fulfill?

Day four with Balak and Balaam and they still don't get it. The king is sure that if he goes to another mountain he will be able to convince the prophet to curse Israel. So they build seven altars and again Balaam says for the king to wait until he goes to find out if he can curse Israel or not.

God speaks to Balaam again, this time in a much stronger tone. I think the text says it best: *"God is not a man, that he should lie, nor a son of man, that he should change his mind. Does he speak and then not act? Does he promise and not fulfill? I have received a command to bless; he has blessed, and I cannot change it."*

Now the king is livid! He tries to get him to curse them again. But this time Balaam gets a glimpse of the entire nation encamped tribe by tribe, at this, he was overwhelmed and began to speak blessing after blessing over Israel.

If God has declared a blessing over you, no man, no enemy can bring a curse on you. Remember that!

Numbers 24:2

When Balaam looked out and saw Israel

We have done over two hundred and seventy days together. Each day I have endeavored to illuminate the Scriptures that Jesus read and bring application to your life. Today I ask that you indulge me to speak of the land of Israel. The text says that when Balaam looked out and saw Israel, the Spirit of the Lord came upon him. Many times as I have stood on a high mountain and overlooked the plains of Israel, I have also felt the presence of God arise.

I have been privileged to go to Israel countless times, and with each trip, I fall more and more in love with the land. The bustling and modern streets of Tel Aviv to the coastal cities of Caesarea, Haifa, and Akko. The calming and stunning view of the Sea of Galilee from the Golan Heights. The vibrant and lush Jordan Valley on the way to the spectacular Dead Sea. And finally, the pearl of the Middle East: Jerusalem.

Let me encourage you, if at all possible, to see the Holy Land for yourself. You'll never be the same again. I can promise you that.

Numbers 25:3

So Israel joined in worshiping the Baal of Peor

Have you ever done something really nice for someone, and not only did he not thank you, but he went out and did something hurtful against you? Can you imagine how that would make you feel? That's how God must have felt in today's passage.

He had rescued His people from slavery, He performed mighty wonders for them, provided for them in the wilderness, protected them from countless enemy attacks, and was delivering them to a Promised Land filled with milk and honey. So how did Israel respond to all this lovingkindness? With betrayal.

No sooner had God protected them from King Balak than the people engaged in all kinds of immoral acts. And the icing on the cake was that they began bowing down to other gods. The Lord's anger burned against them, and rightfully so.

Think of all that God has done for you. Don't cast Him aside at the sight of a shiny new god.

Micah 5:9

*Your hand will be lifted up in triumph
over your enemies*

The book of Micah is classified as one of the Minor Prophets. His audience was that of the southern kingdom of Judah. If you will remember, the nation of Israel was divided: Judah to the south and Israel to the north.

Even at the time of Micah, the Israelites were being oppressed. It's been the story of their lives. As soon as they defeat one nation, another one is in the wings ready to pounce on the weakened state. Though God had declared time and time again that enemies would come up against Israel, He also declared that it would never fall.

Over the centuries, the Jewish people have been scattered all over the world, forced to leave at the hands of others. But in recent years we have been witnessing nothing short of a miracle. From the birth of the nation in 1948 to the incredible victories of the Six Day War and on and on.

Micah's prophecies came true: Israel has triumphed over her enemies. That means that you will too.

Numbers 27:16

Appoint a man over this community

Again in today's passage we see the pattern of succession. There is an interesting change to the pattern here. With Aaron and the priesthood, the mantle was mandated by God and only his sons would be able to carry on the role. It could never be passed on to anyone else. But here, the mantle is passed on to the one that Moses felt was the man that God had chosen.

Joshua was a young man who was filled with the Spirit of God. If you go back to the beginning of the journey of the Israelites, you will recall that Joshua was one of the group who was sent out to spy on the land of Canaan. And it was also Joshua, with Caleb, who came back with a positive report to the people about possessing the land. When he came back from Canaan, little did he know that he would be the one who would be leading the people across the river into the Promised Land.

Joshua was faithful all those years to Moses. He never sought the position, but God raised him up at the appointed time.

Numbers 28:16

The Lord's Passover is to be held

I like the way the Bible titles this feast: the Lord's Passover. It's not called the Feast of the Jews or of Moses, but it's the Lord's Feast. This book is called *What Would Jesus Read?* Years ago there was a famous slogan "What Would Jesus Do?" He would and did celebrate the Passover every year.

Many may think that the feasts in the Old Testament are only for the Jewish people. In light of that assumption, let this verse be food for thought: Numbers 9:14—*"An alien living among you who wants to celebrate the Lord's Passover must do so in accordance with its rules and regulations. You must have the same regulations for the alien and the native-born."*

Celebrating the Passover is not only a command, it's an annual reminder of the incredible things that God did for His people. It's a source of encouragement throughout the ages. It reminds us that God always hears our cries and that He will go to great lengths to secure our freedom. That's something worth celebrating.

Numbers 29:1

It is a day for you to sound the trumpets

The Feast of Trumpets had many significant meanings for the people of the time. First, we need to correctly identify what trumpet was being used. There were silver trumpets that came much later, but at the beginning the trumpet was a ram's horn, also known as a shofar. In fact, if you go back to Exodus 19:16 when the people heard the trumpet blast, the original word in the Hebrew language is shofar. As a result, the shofar has always been associated with the voice of God.

Remember when Joshua and the priests blew the trumpets at Jericho and the walls fell down? They fell because the city trembled when they heard the voice of the Lord. What walls need to fall down in your life? Is there something holding you back from moving on in God?

So on the Feast of Trumpets when the shofars are sounded, it's as if God is speaking to His people. Next time the Feast of Trumpets comes around, ask God to speak to you.

Numbers 29:7

You must deny yourselves

Earlier in this devotional we talked about the Day of Atonement when we were reading through Leviticus 23. I've said it many times, when God decides to repeat something in the Scriptures, it's there for a reason and it deserves our attention.

The Day of Atonement was a special day for the high priest. It was the one and only day in the entire calendar year where he was allowed to go into the Holy of Holies without being struck down by God. Imagine what a sacred and important day that must have been for him. It was a small room. In it was the Ark of the Covenant, where the glory and presence of God used to dwell. There was a thick veil that divided the inner chamber and thus separated him from the presence of God.

How can we as believers today celebrate this feast? Well, first of all, it's the only feast that is a fast. That's why the text says to deny yourselves. It was a time to take the focus off the physical man and center in on the spiritual man.

Numbers 29:12

Celebrate a festival to the LORD for seven days

The Feast of Tabernacles is the longest of the feasts that God told the people to observe. It was a joyous holiday because it commemorated the end of the harvest, and it was a way of thanking God for the provision of the season.

It also was the last festival in the cycle of seven. There were numerous traditions associated with this celebration. One of them was associated with the dedication of the first Temple by King Solomon. According to 2 Chronicles 7:1—on the last and greatest day of this feast, the glory of God filled the Temple.

Another powerful ceremony that took place during Tabernacles was known as the Water Libation Ceremony. This involved drawing water from the pool of Siloam and pouring it onto the altar as a sign of asking God for rain.

It's interesting to note that Jesus celebrated and attended both of these ceremonies according to the New Testament Gospel records.

Numbers 30:1

He must not break his word but must do everything he said

In biblical times, when you gave your word to someone, it was as strong as a legally binding agreement. Things were not just said in passing. But you would think long and hard before you entered into a covenant with someone.

Throughout the Torah verbal agreements and contracts were put in place, and the people who made them would rather die than be accused of not keeping their word.

I can still remember as a kid, my dad would buy a car without a signed contract. A promise meant something. Your word was your bond. As people of faith, we need to be true to what we say. If you make a promise or give your word, do all that you need to do to ensure that you can make it happen.

The world is looking for people who keep their promises. As believers, we have the greatest of examples: the Lord. When God makes a promise, you can take it to the bank. Speak the truth, declare what is right, and honor the Lord and others by keeping your word.

1 Kings 19:12

And after the fire came a gentle whisper

Today's prophetic portion comes from the life of the prophet Elijah. Elijah had the showdown on Mount Carmel with the prophets of Baal. He proved once and for all that the God of Israel was the one and only true God. Next thing you know, he's running scared and running for his life. The king's wife, Jezebel, made a threat against him and the prophet ran. Seems kind of odd, doesn't it? He boldly faced the king and all his false prophets, but he ran at the threat of a woman. Then he sat down under a tree and prayed that he would die!

God met with him and told him that He, the Lord, was about to pass by. First came a powerful wind that tore through the mountains, but God wasn't in it. Then a massive earthquake, but He wasn't in that either. Then came fire—surely God was in the fire, especially after what happened at Mount Carmel—but no, He wasn't there either. Then after the fire came a gentle whisper...and God was in it. You see, that's what Elijah needed, the quiet, comforting voice of God. You may want the fire, but sometimes you need the whisper.

Numbers 31:2

After that, you will be gathered to your people

I don't know how Moses did it. How he continued to serve and fight for God even though he knew he was about to die and would never step foot in the Promised Land. Yet he faithfully served until his dying breath. What an honorable thing to do.

The text says that Moses was going to be gathered to his people. That's the Bible's way of saying you were about to die. It was referring to an ancient burial practice. When people died, they were laid in a cave. Once the body had fully decomposed, the bones of the deceased were gathered up and transferred to the family tomb in their homeland. We saw this in the life of Abraham and then later with Joseph.

How would you respond to an order from someone who just told you that you were going to die and that you wouldn't see the benefit of your labor? Would you do it anyway, because it was the right thing to do? Our responsibility is to do what is right before God. Leave the rest with Him.

Numbers 31:8

*They also killed Balaam son of Beor
with the sword*

I found this verse rather interesting. As I was reading the story of the battle of Israel against the Midianites, a name caught my attention. There was a list of people who were killed in the battle. In verse 8, Balaam son of Beor is listed among the casualties. Does that name ring a bell? Just two weeks ago we spent four days talking about Balaam and his dealings with Balak, the king of Moab. You know what I have learned? That sometimes life just isn't fair. This is the prophet who would not curse Israel. Remember how the king tried to bribe him with silver to curse Israel, but God kept telling him not to? This is the man who has now been killed in battle against Israel.

Hang on…drop down to verse 16. It turns out that it was Balaam who taught the Midianites to worship the Baals, and it was the Midianites who lured Israel into worshiping false gods, and as a result, God sent a plague that killed many people.

Numbers 32:23 says, "And you may be sure your sin will find you out." It seems justice was served.

Numbers 32:7

Why do you discourage the Israelites from going over into the land?

The nation of Israel was at the edge of the Promised Land, literally on the edge. All they had to do was cross the Jordan River and they would be there. Keep in mind that the Jordan was significantly smaller than the Red Sea.

But some of the men wanted to stay on the safe side of the river. Moses was upset and asked them why they insisted on discouraging the people from crossing over. "If you don't want to cross over, that's one thing, but don't ruin it for everyone else." I'm paraphrasing of course, but I don't think I'm too far off. Have you ever met people like that? They don't want to do something, so everyone else has to suffer along with them.

Did you ever play ball hockey or soccer on the street? There was always the one kid who had the ball, and if he didn't get his way or if he didn't want to play anymore, he would take the ball with him. That's the same attitude here. Be a facilitator and not a discourager. Don't let your insecurities be somebody else's downfall.

Jeremiah 1:5

Before I formed you in the womb I knew you

This is probably one of the most quoted verses in the Bible. I challenge you to walk into a Christian bookstore and not find a greeting card or a framed picture with his verse on it. It is such a loved verse, and with reason. The thought of God being with us in the womb is so precious and comforting.

Some people struggle with personal identity all their lives. They're never quite sure who they are or what they have been called to do in this life. Maybe you're reading this today, and you're that person. Let me encourage you, not with my words, but with the words of the living God. You were no accident. If you're alive and you are on this planet, then there is a purpose for your life.

Your only responsibility is to discover what that purpose is and then live it out to the best of your ability. Don't worry if you haven't found it yet. If you keep seeking, you will find it. And once you do find it, it will be the most rewarding feeling you have ever experienced.

Jeremiah 1:7

*But the L*ORD *said to me, "Do not say,*
'I am only a child'"

When you're young, you want to look older. When you're older, you want to look younger. People are never quite happy where they are. The truth is that you have to be comfortable in your skin.

We have already had a devotional talking about the importance of respecting the elderly. I stressed the importance of this younger generation respecting the seniors of our community. Now I want to turn the tables and stress to the seniors and to the older crowd that you also need to respect and pray for the young people! You need to understand that if a generation isn't mentoring and training up young people to be future leaders, then that generation is doomed to fade away.

Consider how Moses mentored Joshua. Let me talk for a moment to my senior readers: invest in the life of a young person. You have valuable life skills and experience that you must pass on to this next generation. We need our young people to rise up and become who God has called them to be, and you can have a role in that.

Jeremiah 1:8

Do not be afraid of them, for I am with you

This is another one of those beautiful promises that God made to His servant Jeremiah. God gave Jeremiah a very difficult calling to accept. Jeremiah wasn't just called to speak in the public square and spout some end-time prophecies. He was called to rebuke kings and nations. That was no small task.

The promise implies that Jeremiah was indeed afraid, and rightly so. When we read some of his prophecies, it's easy to imagine a bold and brave prophet, declaring God's wrath and judgment. He may have turned out that way, but I don't think that was always the case.

We have this idea that all men and women of God were innately brave or natural-born leaders. Abraham was a small-business owner, Joseph was a dreamer, and Moses had a speech impediment.

If God has called you, then God will equip you. You only need to stand up and allow Him to mold you.

Jeremiah 1:9

Now, I have put my words in your mouth

Many of you may not believe what I'm about to say. Growing up, I was the shyest kid you could ever meet. I despised public attention. I went through most of my life completely unnoticed, and I was happy about it. I remember once in elementary school, when it was time for public speeches, I pretended to be sick so I wouldn't have to stand up in front of the class. Pretending to be sick wasn't too far from the truth—I would have become sick if I had to get up and speak.

Even in my first year at seminary, I was afraid to death of public speaking. I remember almost getting sick to my stomach the first time I had to speak in front of my peers. You may find all that hard to believe, but it's the honest truth. Now I make my living by public speaking, not just to small crowds in churches, but now to millions of people via television. What changed? Like Jeremiah, God reached out and touched my mouth and gave me a message to speak. Don't be afraid. Speak the words He has given you and everything will work out just fine...trust me!

Numbers 33:2

*At the Lord's command Moses recorded the stages
in their journey*

Life is the most exciting journey you will ever take. There are both good and bad times, highs and lows, but in the end, it's worth it all. It's nice to get together with friends and recount some great trip or experience. I don't know what stage of life you're in, but I find that as I get older, the details aren't as sharp as they used to be!

Sometimes my wife and I will be talking about somewhere that we recently went, and though it may have been days before, it seems to me like it was months ago. That's why it's so important to write things down. That way you can easily go back and remember what you did or said.

That's what God has Moses do. Before more time passed on, God commanded Moses to write down everything that had happened to the Israelites. Could you imagine what a loss it would have been if Moses didn't remember the details of the Exodus? What a loss for humanity that would have been. Take some time and start today. Write down the important things so you can look back and remember.

Numbers 33:3

They marched out boldly in full view of all the Egyptians

I love the way the text remembers the day that the Israelites left Egypt. It says that they boldly walked away from their taskmasters with confidence. They didn't have to run away like scared little children. They knew who their God was and what He had done for them in setting them free. You think of a prison break and how fast the inmates would run if they were given a window of opportunity to escape. But not the children of Israel—when they walked out, they walked out with their heads held high. Their time of shame had come to an end. They were now a free people. I love it!

Remember when you were a slave to sin before God set you free? Remember the shame you felt as you continually struggled to loosen its grip on your life? But then you found your salvation and refuge in God. Now you know who you are in Him. You're a King's kid! No one can take that away from you. Walk humbly before God in the freedom that He has provided for you, but walk boldly in the presence of your enemy. He also remembers what your God did for you.

Numbers 35:12

They will be places of refuge from the avenger

This is truly an amazing biblical concept put in place by God to protect His people. They were known as the cities of refuge. There were six in total and were scattered throughout the region. These cities were set up so anyone who had killed someone accidentally would have a place to run to where his avenger would not be able to get to him.

Three were set up on the Canaan side and three on the east side of the Jordan. This is the great part about the whole thing: the cities weren't only for God's people, they were also for anyone in the region. Once you were within its fortified walls, you were untouchable.

Is it any wonder that the Bible is filled with verses that refer to God as a refuge in times of trouble? You have to view those Scriptures in light of the time and place that they were written. When they called God their refuge, they had these six cities in mind. Run to Him today; let Him be your refuge so your accuser can't lay a hand on you!

Numbers 35:26

But if the accused ever goes outside the limits of
the city of refuge

I spend a good amount of time in Israel. One of my greatest memories is when I got to play shepherd one afternoon. I was given a staff and a flock of sheep, and was told to drive them from one side of a field to the other. I noticed that the more time I spent with them, the more they listened. As long as they were in my presence, they were protected.

Flocks of sheep would be the equivalent of a bank account today. Sheep and other livestock were the currency of the day, so you would protect them with your very life. As long as the sheep were with the shepherd, they would be safe. But if one got out and was in the open, it would be fair game for wolves and wild desert animals.

It was the same principle with the cities of refuge. You were safe while within its walls, but if you left, your accuser had the right to kill you without penalty. It's the same with God. Like a sheep, if you stay close to Him you will be protected. But if you run, you are at risk of being attacked. Stay close to Him.

Jeremiah 2:5

*What fault did your fathers find in me, that they
strayed so far?*

The prophecy in today's passage is more of a lament.
Through the prophet Jeremiah, God looks back to the
time of the Exodus and recounts His relationship with
His people. The memories start off fondly enough, but
then quickly turn to their abandonment.

God talks about how committed the people were to
Him. He even goes as far as to compare His relationship
with them to a newly married couple. He's referring back
to the time when He was their first love. But then the
mood sharply changes. God is asking why the sudden
change of heart; why did His people turn from Him? I
know that there are many people who are asking similar
questions about relationships and friendships that they
have had in the past. At first everything was fine and then,
without warning, everything changed.

God wants you to go back to the time when He was
your everything. Like a forgiving husband, He is calling
us back to fellowship with Him. Let Him restore your
relationship to how it used to be.

Jeremiah 2:20

Long ago you broke off your yoke

Here's the word "yoke" again. It's so unfortunate that in the Christian context this word has taken on a negative meaning. That having a yoke tied around your neck was a bad thing. I know that we have talked about this before, but it bears having a quick review. Yokes were seen as very important tools in the success or failure of your crops. They were used to keep the oxen on a straight path so the seeds could be planted and the harvest would grow properly.

If the rows were not straight, then the crops would grow into one another and become entangled, eventually suffocating the plants, and there would be no harvest! In this verse, God was upset because they took off their yokes. He wasn't upset because He had somehow lost His ability to control them. But He knew that without His yoke—His laws—the people would go astray and lose their way.

Please, wear the yoke God has given you. It will keep you on the straight and narrow path. It's not a method of control; it's His way of protecting you.

Jeremiah 2:27

When they are in trouble, they say,
"Come and save us!"

I had a good chuckle as I was preparing to write this devotional today. It conjures up images in my mind that I know many of you will be able to relate to. For those who have children, or even if you babysit, you'll understand this example. Have you ever tried to help a toddler between the ages of two and three? Good luck! That's the defiant stage of independence. They want to do *everything* for themselves, but they can't...and you have to let them try.

It can be feeding themselves, tying their shoes, or riding a bike. As soon as you offer to help, they sternly let you know that they don't need your help. But inevitably they fall or spill something or something goes wrong. And as soon as they fail, they are quick to ask for your help.

That's what God is saying here about His people. They didn't want His laws or help, but as soon as they were in trouble they cried out for His help. And like a loving parent, He reached out His hand.

Deuteronomy 1:6

You have stayed long enough at this mountain

Forty years had now passed from the time of the Exodus. A lot had happened in that time period. There were some highs and some definite lows. But nonetheless, Moses was preparing the people for the final crossing into the Promised Land. The book of Deuteronomy is Moses' memoirs. It's a look back on their forty-year journey. Many times he reminded them of past events.

Moses reminded them of the day God ordered them to leave the mountain. Moses had a lot of personal history with Mount Horeb. Go back to the very beginning of his journey with the Israelites. It was at this mountain that he saw the burning bush and where he was commissioned by the Lord to lead the people out of Egypt. It was also here that he provided water from the rock. Moses had some good memories here. It was probably a place of comfort to him.

You see, if we stay in our comfort zones, then we'll never make it to the Promised Land. Go and make new memories in God! When God says it is time, leave the mountain.

Deuteronomy 1:12

But how can I bear your problems . . .
all by myself?

Remember that the book of Deuteronomy is a recap of the entire Exodus experience. Moses will die soon, as God had told him. He needed to preserve the Law and the details of their wandering. It must have been an amazing experience to tell some of the stories again. Remember that it has been forty years since the Exodus. An entire generation had risen up who had not been part of the Exodus. I wonder what it must have been like for them to hear the stories their parents had told them, but this time from Moses himself.

As he looks back on his experience he remembers how overwhelmed he was at first when the responsibility of all the people was dropped in his lap. I can't imagine the pressure he must have faced every day. Can you imagine how much food and water was necessary to feed six hundred thousand people every day for forty years?

He learned that in order to successfully manage all the people, he had to rely on the help of others as well. Don't be a hero; share the burden.

Deuteronomy 1:25

*It is a good land that the L*ORD *our*
God is giving us

Today Moses is remembering the day that he sent out the spies to Canaan, the Promised Land. Just put yourself in their position for a minute if you can. They had been set free from a grueling and miserable existence as slaves. They walked through the intense heat of the Sinai Desert for years at a time, and now they were about to get a report of the land where they were going.

I liken it to a bride and groom. You make all the plans for the wedding day. All the guests have arrived, the food is all ready, and the church is full. As the groom, you're at the front of the church waiting to see your bride. You know what she looks like, but you can't wait to see her on that day in her wedding gown.

When the spies returned, they had fruit that was so big that it took two men and a pole to carry a single cluster of grapes. It was more than the people expected. The Lord your God wants to give you a good land, a good place. Step out and follow Him on the most amazing journey of your life.

Deuteronomy 1:31

As a father carries his son

We've talked about the Israelites leaving their comfort zone to begin a journey to the Promised Land. We have seen all the wars and trials the people faced as they trusted God through their experience. We spent a lot of time reviewing their grumblings and their complaints. It's so easy for us today to judge their actions.

The people had it rough in Egypt, but let's be honest: the journey to the Promised Land was no picnic. I think most people have this idealistic view that their journey in God will be all perfect and they won't have any problems. The truth is that the journey can be difficult, but the prize is worth the price.

Moses began to comfort the people. Even though they had disobeyed God and had aroused His anger, He still loved them and kept His promises to them. He said that God carried them as a father carries his son. How many of you parents have carried a sleeping child from the car to bed? Have that image in your mind as you read about their journeys. He carries us when we are weak.

Deuteronomy 2:19

When you come to the Ammonites, do not harass them or provoke them to war

You have to know when to fight and when to step back. That was the situation for Israel. They were a developing nation of former slaves. They had no formal training in war. All they had were their survival skills. In the natural, they were no match for the Amorites and other fully developed and militarized nations.

The only strength they had was the Lord. I know that's all they needed, but they could only go to war if He was with them. If He told them to go, then their victory was secured. But if they were proud and arrogant, thinking their victories were because of how great they were, and God did not go with them, then they would surely lose.

It's the same way with us. We may not be talking about a physical war, but many times people and situations come against us. We need to be in proper fellowship with the commander, the Lord. We can only go when He tells us to go. We can't do it without Him. Wait on God.

Deuteronomy 3:22

Do not be afraid of them; the Lord your God himself will fight for you

When you're going through a battle in your life, it's difficult to get perspective sometimes. All you can see is the war in front of you. You don't know if you're five hundred meters from the Promised Land or five hundred miles! Only after everything is done are you able to look back and see things for the way they really were. Remember that in the book of Deuteronomy, Moses is reflecting and passing on to the next generation the history of what happened to them over the past forty years.

When you're sitting in the shade with food in your belly, it's hard to appreciate the severity of the war you're hearing about. Moses is reminding them of what God did and what He said to them in times of war. God told Moses and Joshua not to fear—again, easier said than done. They were up against some pretty tough people. But knowing that God was on their side gave them the confidence and the peace to know that they would succeed. God will fight for you, but you have to let Him lead. Follow Him and you will be just fine.

Words **307**

Isaiah 1:18

Though your sins are like scarlet, they shall be as white as snow

Isaiah is one of the most read books of the Old Testament. This particular text strikes a chord with people because of the nature of its power. The thought that God could take people who are such sinners, stained with the stench of sin, and forgive them is a comforting thought.

Did you know that this passage is associated with an awesome practice from the time of the Tabernacle in the wilderness? It actually comes from an ancient ceremony connected to the Day of Atonement. Jewish literature tells about this practice. The priest would tie a scarlet-colored thread to the head of the goat that was released into the wilderness, and then later on it was pushed off a cliff (see Week 29, Day 3). As the goat fell, the scarlet thread would turn white, signifying that the Lord had accepted the sacrifice and forgiven the sins of the people. Pretty cool, right?

We can experience the same forgiving power of God in our lives today. We can go boldly before His throne and ask for His forgiveness.

Deuteronomy 3:25

Let me go over and see the good land

Moses knew that he would not be entering the Promised Land. He had already accepted that fact long ago. But as the time drew closer to the crossing, Moses began to get restless with the idea. The ban to not cross had happened so long ago that it went to the back of his mind.

We do the same thing Moses did, just in a different context. Have you ever committed to something that you really didn't want to do, but because it was so far in the future you said yes? That's kind of how it was with Moses.

Although he was at peace with the consequence, he still wanted at the very least to see the Promised Land. He literally pesters God until He says yes. Pestering God is a foreign concept to us, I know, but in Judaism it is an accepted way of approaching Him. God allows him to go up and see the land. It must have been a bittersweet moment for him. He was so excited to see the Promised Land for his people, but bitter because he knew he would not step foot in it. That's why it's so important to obey God.

Deuteronomy 4:7

What other nation is so great as to have their gods near them the way the Lord our God is near us whenever we pray to him?

We have to be careful not to take our relationship with God for granted. We should also be grateful for the freedom that we have to approach our God anytime we want. Had you ever considered how difficult it is in other religions to approach their deity? Some can't even talk to their god unless they perform some extensive ritual to invoke speaking rights. Some religions hold their gods in such high esteem that they are too lofty to communicate with mere mortals. Only in Judaism and Christianity do we serve a God who is as close to us as a simple prayer. All we have to do is speak His name and He is there. In fact, He knows what our words will be before we even utter them.

Moses is reminding them how great their relationship with God is. None of the nations around them enjoyed the same privilege. Just as Moses reminded the people, allow me to remind you again: Who is like our God? What other people can call on His name and He will answer? We serve a great and mighty God!

Deuteronomy 4:29

You will find him if you seek him
with all your heart

In this passage Moses was encouraging the Israelites, as he had done many times before, not to go after the false gods that they would encounter in the Promised Land. He reminded them of how foolish it is to pray to man-made idols made of wood and stone. They cannot hear you nor can they speak.

He tells them that their God is the only God who can communicate with them. If you seek Him with all your heart, you will find Him. Even Jesus refers to this passage during His ministry. We need to remind ourselves that, as a devout Jew, Jesus was reading these weekly passages, and they undoubtedly found their way into his sermons.

We find what we seek. So what or who are you seeking? Are you going after the material things of this world? If so, they are only temporary and will do you no good in eternity. Are you seeking the Lord and His will for your life? If you are, then you are investing in eternity. Seek Him and you will find Him. He wants to be found; all we have to do is look.

Deuteronomy 5:32

Do not turn aside to the right or to the left

Today's passage is a review of the Ten Commandments. Moses reiterates them to all the people. I get chills when I read them today. Can you imagine what it was like to be sitting on a hillside with Moses, with the actual tablets in his hand, listening to him read them out loud? Wow, talk about an amazing sermon!

Where do you begin a review of the Ten Commandments? Entire books can and have been written on each one. But the one line that really caught my attention was about not turning to the right or left—that you must follow His commandments exactly. One wrong move and we fall. Think of tightrope walkers. With extreme focus and concentration they look straight ahead. One sudden turn or misstep and it's game over.

This takes us back to the yoke; remember, it helps us keep true north. God's commandments are the yoke that assure us eternity. Even though it's tempting to look sometimes, we have to keep our eyes on the prize.

Deuteronomy 6:4

*Hear O Israel: The L*ORD *our God, the L*ORD *is one*

In Hebrew, this is called the Shema or Sh'ma. It is one of the central prayers in Judaism and is at the very heart of Jewish doctrine. This idea is what separated and still separates Judaism from many other world religions. Many groups believed in a plethora of deities. The ancient peoples had altars built in every fortified city. These altars were dedicated to the many gods to which they prayed.

Some of us can be quick to judge these ancient and backward people. They didn't know any better, is what you might say. Well then, what's our excuse today? We're so advanced with all our technology and have apparently morally evolved into a better species, yet we worship all kinds of false idols today. You can say "ouch" or "amen"— the choice is yours.

We may not build altars and have statues in our homes or churches, but we certainly do lift up people and things to places where they don't belong. Let me rephrase the text from today: Hear O Christian, the Lord our God, the Lord is one!

Deuteronomy 7:9

Keeping his covenant of love to a thousand generations

I get mixed emotions when I read this passage. The first part of the text talks about Israel completely destroying seven stronger nations, as commanded by God. The second part of the text breaks into this beautiful language used by God to describe His feelings about Israel.

Why does God tell Israel to completely destroy the seven cities that are mentioned in the text? We sometimes have a tough time understanding how God can be so loving on the one hand and then so brutal on the other. I know that even talking about this makes some people uncomfortable, but there must be a reason why God acts the way He does. Of course there is a good reason. The nations that were being called to destruction were the seven cities that not only served false gods, but they had lured the Israelites into doing the same.

God wanted them wiped out so His people would not go astray again. It's like when a lioness kills another animal to protect her own. No one messes with God's kids!

Isaiah 40:1–2

Comfort, comfort my people, says your God.
Speak tenderly to Jerusalem

The view of God in the Old Testament is usually that of an angry and judgmental God. Just yesterday we talked about the fact that sometimes God roars like a lion and destroys His enemies in order to protect His people. Today's passage from the prophets beautifully picks up on this idea of God loving His people.

The text starts with a command from God for us to comfort His people, to speak gently to them. The image that immediately popped into my head was that of a new-born baby. With older children, you can throw them up in the air and roughhouse with them. But with babies, you have to tenderly hold their heads up and speak softly around them so as not to frighten them.

Israel was God's baby. He brought the nation out of slavery and into the Promised Land. But they were a new people, a baby nation if you will.

God says that He will bless those who bless His people. Let us speak tenderly to Jerusalem.

Deuteronomy 7:21

Do not be terrified by them, for the LORD
*your God, who is among you, is a great and
awesome God*

The children of Israel were a relatively small group of people. They had been freed from slavery for less than forty years, and now God was asking them to fight and defeat other nations who were much bigger and stronger. They were afraid. But then comes verse 21: *"Do not be terrified by them, for the* LORD *your God, who is among you, is a great and awesome God!"* What has God asked you to do that you are afraid to do? What excuses have you come up with? Maybe there are more-qualified people around you for that job. Perhaps you feel like you are not a natural-born leader.

The truth is that it doesn't matter what the circumstances are. If God calls you, rest assured that He will give you what is necessary to complete the task. Someone once said, "God doesn't call the qualified, He qualifies the called." So what dream, vision, or passion have you left to collect dust on the proverbial shelf? Always remember what the Torah says: "You serve a great and awesome God!"

Deuteronomy 8:11

*Be careful that you do not forget the LORD
your God*

A land flowing with milk and honey and a land filled with plenty—that is what God promised the Israelites. He promised to meet all their needs with every kind of provision imaginable. He also warned them not to forget that it was He, the Lord, who had done it. Even though God had done so much for the people of Israel, they were quick to forget the Lord.

What about you? What are you like when things are going well? Is your business growing? Is your church bursting at the seams? Perhaps your bank account and belly are both full. Have you forgotten the Lord in your time of plenty? It's easy to think that our success is because of us. God says, "Don't forget me." He wants to remind you that it was He who provided for you in the desert. He's the one who brought manna from heaven and water from a rock. It was He who brought you into a land filled with blessing. It's easy to remember and turn to God when things are tough. But it is easy to forget Him when times are good.

Thank Him, Bless Him . . . never forget Him.

Deuteronomy 9:7

*Remember this and never forget how you
provoked the Lord your God to anger
in the desert*

Doesn't this command to remember the story of the golden calf seem a little obvious? I love how Moses just kind of brings it up. "Don't you ever forget what you did in the desert on the day you made a false idol," Moses says. "While I was up on the mountain with God, getting the Law for you so you could be a people, you were down there breaking the command before I even had a chance to show it to you." (Paraphrased, of course.)

How could the people forget? I don't think they could. God's anger burned so fiercely that the earth opened up and began swallowing people. And then God commanded that three thousand more people be put to death because it was such a horrible offense.

Sometimes we like to downgrade the level of our sin. We reason with ourselves and say that it's not that bad. Who do we think we're kidding? God is a loving God, but He is also a jealous God. There are many false gods, but only one true God. Adonai!

Deuteronomy 10:1

*Chisel out two stone tablets like the first ones
and come up to me*

Moses is reminding Israel about some of the events that had happened over the past forty years. Here we are reminded that Israel was not chosen because of its perfection or abilities, but because God is a covenant-keeping God. Moses spent forty days and forty nights without eating and drinking as he was receiving the Ten Commandments. He reminds the people how they were quick to turn from God and how they had broken one of the commandments at Mount Sinai by making the golden calf.

He recounts how it was God who initiated a second issuing of the Ten Commandments, that it was the Lord who reached out to Israel. How many times have we failed the Lord by disobeying His commandments? Have you ever done something that was so bad—I mean really bad—you felt like God could never forgive you? Be reminded of His lovingkindness today. Just like God told Moses to come up to Him, He's telling you the same thing. He loves you, and He wants to restore you.

Deuteronomy 10:12

What does the LORD your God ask of you?

Today's text asks a great question. What does the Lord our God expect of us? Is He looking for a perfect people? Is He looking for followers who never make mistakes? No. He is looking for a people who will fear Him and will do all they can to walk in His ways. He wants us to love Him with our whole heart.

Some people have either walked away from the faith or have chosen never to come near it because they feel that they are unworthy. They feel like they can never measure up to God's standard. He's not looking for a perfect person, just for someone who has a heart after Him. Do you remember King David? He is held up as one of the greatest Bible heroes ever. Even the Messiah is called the Son of David. This David must have been a perfect human being in order to be so esteemed by God. Yeah, right! David was as flawed as you and I are.

Don't walk away from God because you feel like you don't measure up. None of us do. That's what makes His love so great.

Deuteronomy 11:24

Every place where you set your foot will be yours

What's the key to a successful life? I suppose the answer depends on who you ask. Some might say that having the right attitude is the key. Others might say that it depends on who you know in the industry that you're trying to make it in. What does the Bible say? That's always a great place to look! That's where we should always go to get our answers.

Moses says that the key to a successful life is honoring God and obeying His commandments. In fact, God says that if you hold fast to Him, He will give you every place where you set your feet. What does it mean to hold fast to something? What is your rock when life tries to wash you away like a rushing river? What's your default safety? Do you turn to an addiction, do you turn to a friend, or do you turn to God?

By holding fast to Him, God also said that He would drive your enemies from you! That means that you don't have to concern yourself with them. You just focus on God, and He'll take care of them.

Isaiah 49:16

*See, I have engraved you on the palms
of my hands*

Did you go away to camp as a kid or have sleepovers at your friends' houses? I used to go to a day camp as a teenager, and when I became a Christian, I used to go away on youth retreats. Did anyone else's mom either sew or write your name on your boots or sleeping bag? It was so embarrassing. I hate to admit it, but it worked. If someone else tried to put on my boots, there was my name, hand stitched on the inside tongue. It was a quick way of identifying what belonged to me.

God says the same thing about you! When you're His, He writes your name on the palm of His hands. It's His way of always remembering that you are His. Isaiah goes on to say that if we call on His name, He will answer.

He can never forget you. Not just because your name is written on His hand, but because He says that in the same way a mother cannot forget her baby, neither can the Lord forget you. You are His. No one can take you from His hand. Be encouraged today and know that you are loved with an everlasting love.

Deuteronomy 11:26

*See, I am setting before you today a blessing
and a curse*

Some people think that we are living in a totally prede-termined robotlike state—that we don't have free will of any kind. How does that make you feel, to think that you don't get a say in the matter? That some celestial being has made all our choices for us, and that we are all some kind of cosmic lab rats? Not a good feeling, right?

I don't buy that sales pitch. It doesn't line up with what I read in the Torah, and certainly not in this passage. Here God is laying a choice before the people, and by exten-sion, to all of us today. He says that He allows us to choose between blessings or curses. We choose between life or death.

That means that I am the one who is responsible for my actions and for the choices I make today. I can't blame my parents or my teachers or my preachers, but me—I choose! That's why I can't blame God when things go wrong in my life. He has made all the provisions. I'm the one who has to choose to apply them to my life. Choose blessing today, choose life, choose God.

Deuteronomy 12:8

*You are not to do as we do here today,
everyone as he sees fit*

What is the one true religion? That's a big question, right? The answer you get will depend on who you talk to. There are so many religions in the world today. Even under the umbrella of the Church, there are so many denominations and variations of Christian practice. But I think the biggest church in the world is the church of "Me."

You know this church; you may even attend there sometimes. We've all attended there from time to time. We know what the Bible says and we know what God wants, but sometimes we just want what we want! That's what the passage today is talking about.

Everyone wanted to do as they saw fit—the old idea that whatever works for you is the right way to go. That doesn't fly with God. In fact, He ordered that all the altars of other gods be torn down. The only way is God's way. We may not always like it, but guess what? Medicine doesn't always taste great either, but it's what you need. We need God!

Deuteronomy 13:4

*It is the L*ORD* your God you must follow*

Fake: A thing that is not genuine; a forgery or sham. In your experience, what qualifies as fake based on this definition? Have you ever received an automated phone call telling you that you have won a free cruise or whatever? All you have to do is give them your credit card number to pay for the tax, and off you go . . . probably a fake.

There were fakes during the biblical period too. God goes to great lengths to warn His people about them. There were prophets who were going around telling people which gods they should worship. The Lord said that if anyone told the Israelites to worship gods other than Him, then that prophet is a fake.

Everybody has the right to choose what religion he wants to follow and which god he wants to serve. A couple of days ago we talked about free will, so you can make your own choice, even the wrong one. Choose the God of Elijah, who answered by fire; choose the God of Israel, who parted the Red Sea. There is only one true God, and His name is the Lord . . . choose Him.

Deuteronomy 14:29

*So that the L*ORD *your God may bless you in all
the work of your hands*

I have a confession to make . . . I want to live a blessed life.
I want my wife and children to live a blessed life. How can I
ensure that they do live a blessed life? That's easy; just follow the Torah's advice in today's passage.

God says that the best way to ensure that He will bless
all the work of my hands is if I bless His house. That
means with my finances. God says that we need to bless
those who work for Him. In this passage He was referring
to the priests, because they were given no allotment of
land. They only lived off what the people brought in to the
Lord for sacrifice.

I want you to be blessed too. There's no secret or magic
formula. God makes it as clear as glass. If you bless His
house, He will bless you. Some people try to make it on
their own steam; they work so hard and yet always fall
short. Let me encourage you to take a leap of faith today.
Give to God and trust Him to supply your every need.

Deuteronomy 15:4

There should be no poor among you

Moses has been recounting to the people what God had already said before. Anyone who has studied for an exam or tried to memorize lines will tell you that the best way to do it is through repetition. Repetition is also key when instructing people. If you say it enough times, people will start to listen. In this portion the passage Moses is reminding them about the year of jubilee.

This happened every fifty years in Israel. Debts were canceled and loans were forgiven. How about reinstating this long-lost Torah gem into our modern-day society? I'm sure that would get a lot of votes. The point of the year of jubilee was to ensure that everyone was on the same playing field when it came to finances.

Whether we like it or not, we treat people based on the level of their income. Even during the sinking of the *Titanic*, the rich got onto the lifeboats first. We as believers are called to be different. In God we are all on equal terms. We need to treat the rich, the poor, and everyone in between with the same grace.

Deuteronomy 16:16

Three times a year all your men must appear
before the LORD your God

I've had many people tell me that the Old Testament no longer has any application for Christians living today— that the New Testament has somehow canceled out the Old Testament. If that's the case, then we've just spent the past 327 days studying an outdated and out-of-service book! I hardly think so. To people who question the validity of the Old Testament, I would challenge them to read it for themselves. Also, answer me this...if the Old Testament is no longer valid, then why did Jesus and every New Testament writer quote from it?

Of course the answer is because it is not outdated or irrelevant. It is filled with the wisdom of God, as we have seen all these days. Granted, some of the practices are no longer possible because the Temple is gone, but the morals and principles are timeless and universal.

Even the command listed in today's passage to practice the feasts—they are annual reminders of all that God has done for us. How can that be outdated or irrelevant?

Isaiah 54:17

No weapon forged against you will prevail

How powerful is this verse? Here is another question—to whom is this promise directed? The right answer is to Israel. Some of you don't agree, but why? Because of a terrible theology that has ravaged the church for centuries. It's called "replacement theology." Many people practice it without even knowing what it is. That's how devious this teaching is. Basically, it says that because Israel rejected Jesus, God rejected Israel. And because of this, every time you see Israel in the Bible, you should replace it with the word "Church"—hence the term replacement theology. The line of thinking is that as long as Israel is mentioned in the context of judgment, it's okay to keep the word Israel there. But whenever it refers to blessing, that now refers to the Church.

How many times in the Bible did God say His covenant with Israel was eternal? I counted 251...give or take a few, depending on your translation. The truth is that the promises for Israel are eternal but some now apply to us as well. We have been grafted into Israel and share in the inheritance!

See **329**

Deuteronomy 17:16

You are not to go back that way again

As Moses continues to walk down memory lane with the people, there are a few bumps along the road. In today's passage a number of topics are being covered. One topic dealt with the sacrifices that the people were allowed to bring to God. It had to be the best—no defects or deformities. Whatever we give to God, it has to be our best. It doesn't always have to be the biggest and most expensive, but the best that we can do.

I found the other topic of great interest. Moses told the people not to go back to Egypt—that they were not allowed to go back down that road. What in the world would the people want to go back to? Remember when they were grumbling? That was the first place they wanted to go.

How many times has someone you know fallen back into his old ways? Even though it may be dangerous and addictive, we tend to return to a place where we felt comfort, even if that means being a slave to it. May God fully deliver us from our past.

Deuteronomy 17:18

Write for himself on a scroll a copy of this law

This was a command for the king of Israel, that he should write down the entire Torah on a scroll for himself. It took Moses more than forty years to live out the Torah. I can't imagine how long it would have taken to write it by hand. They only had scrolls and basic dipping pens; it would have taken years to write it all down. I think that was the whole point of the exercise. As the king wrote it, it would go not only into his mind, but also into his heart.

Today we can go online to a Bible website, hit Copy and Paste, and then click the Print icon, and in a few minutes we can have whatever part of the Bible we want. That definitely wasn't the case back then.

Earlier we talked about journaling, about writing down the significant things that God has done for you. Have you started? If so, how's it going? Along with writing, let me also encourage you to read every day. It can be from the Torah, the Prophets, or wherever you choose. The more you get it in you, the more it will come out of you in your daily life.

Deuteronomy 18:9

*Do not learn to imitate the detestable ways
of the nations*

Have you ever heard the phrase "monkey see, monkey do"? That's what God was talking about in this passage. The Israelites were about to enter into the Promised Land, and based on their previous track record, the Lord was justified in being concerned that they would just jump on the bandwagon and start doing what everyone else was doing.

Today we call it peer pressure. Everyone thinks that it only applies to high school, but it actually carries on for the rest of your life. Everywhere you go, people will constantly challenge your faith. It doesn't matter if you work in a doctor's office or a warehouse...peer pressure is there.

Sometimes peer pressure manifests itself in an invitation to go to a particular social event, or it can be to condone a certain lifestyle. People just want you to blend in and be like them.

But that's not our calling as the people of God. We are called to be a shining light in an ever-increasingly dark world.

Deuteronomy 19:14

Do not move your neighbor's boundary stone

The Israelites were about to come into a whole new land. All of it was theirs for the taking. God promised the entire land of Canaan to them. It seems odd that the Lord would tell them not to move their neighbor's boundary stone. In today's terms, that would be the equivalent of a property line or a fence line. More relationships have been ruined by putting up fences in backyards than we can imagine. You know what I'm talking about. It has wrecked friendships and even caused people to move.

So why is God giving the people instructions about not moving property lines? You see, it came down to the issue of honesty and integrity. When your neighbor was out doing whatever it was that she was doing, you could have easily moved the stones over a few feet and nobody would be the wiser.

So is it only wrong if you get caught? Or is it wrong because it's wrong? That's the issue that God was dealing with. It doesn't matter who is or who isn't looking. God sees, and He's the only one that matters.

Deuteronomy 20:8

Is any man afraid or fainthearted?
Let him go home

God also gave the people instructions for war, which was a constant reality in those days. If you wanted someone's land, you fought him. If you won, you took his land. That was that. It was the accepted way to expand your territory, and all the nations of the time practiced it.

Many times, if not every time, the Israelites were going up against bigger and better armies. And each time, God's response was the same. That if He had called them, He would go before them and they would win. On this particular occasion, some new exceptions were introduced. They had to do with dedicating a home or being engaged to be married. If so, you could be excused from battle. A new exception was: if you were scared, go home. Just like that.

God's looking for people who are not afraid of the enemy, a people who are willing to fight for what is right. It takes courage to confront the darkness of this world, but with God on our side, the victory is secure.

Isaiah 51:1

Look to the rock from which you were cut

It's often been said that the apple doesn't fall far from the tree. I'm sure you've heard that expression. Or what about "he's a chip off the old block"? I'm sure you've heard that one too. They both mean the same thing—that you're not that different from your parents.

In Isaiah, God creates His own saying to make the same point. He says, "Look to the rock from which you were cut and to the quarry from which you were hewn." Then He proceeds to tell us who we are like. He's not talking about your earthly parents here but your spiritual father: Abraham.

God wants us to be like some of the characters of old. Abraham was an obedient man who came from humble beginnings. But because he obeyed God, he became the father of us all. We could add to this list. For the men, we could be more like Joseph, Moses, or Joshua. For the ladies, you could be more like Sarah, Rachel, or Deborah. The point is that we have a great spiritual heritage that we can tap into when looking for someone to model after.

Isaiah 51:4

The law will go out from me; my justice will become a light to the nations

What was the purpose of God to give Israel the Law? He knew from the start that they would not be able to keep it, so why give it to them in the first place? Because the Law was not just for them. God chose the Jewish people from the nations of the earth to be His people, that's true. But they were chosen, not preferred. We have to remember that. Being the chosen people came at a terrible price. History shows us all too well the price the Jews have paid.

They carry a huge burden, which is to be a light to the nations. They were chosen to receive and preserve His Law. They were to study it, live it, and ultimately they were to share it with others around them.

The same can be said of us. Our role is to internalize God's commands and then live them so that others may see. The first set of laws were written on tablets of stone, but God's true intention is to have His Law written on our hearts, that we may be a living example of what it represents.

Deuteronomy 21:21

You must purge the evil from among you

Have you noticed that mankind seems to have an obsession with evil? We always seem to want what we can't or shouldn't have. Where do we get that from? The Bible teaches that we are all born with evil inclination that stems from the sin of Adam and Eve. Have you ever wondered what our world would be like if they hadn't given in to the serpent's temptation?

I guess we'll never know. This is the world we live in and this is the world that we have. There is no other alternative this side of heaven. All we can do is strive to live a life that is holy and pleasing to God.

The text says that we have to purge the evil from among us. In the context of the passage it was dealing with a rebellious son. But it can definitely be applied more broadly here. How do we get rid of the evil that is in each of us? The sad truth is that we can't totally get rid of it; it's something that we will struggle with all our lives. But with God's grace and help, we can live victorious lives.

Deuteronomy 22:1

If you see your brother's ox or sheep straying,
do not ignore it

Not too many of us can relate to this command in its most literal sense. Some may live on a farm and may actually see their neighbor's ox or sheep run astray, but most of us will not get the chance to see that happen.

Again, this is one of those passages that can be applied in a much broader sense. The principle is universal: if you see people going astray, don't ignore them, do what you can to get them back on track!

Remember what Cain said to God way back at the beginning of Genesis? "Am I my brother's keeper?" The answer is a resounding yes! When you signed on and became a believer, you became part of a much bigger family, a much bigger world, than just that of yourself. We are bound by love to help one another. Whether they are part of your church or synagogue is irrelevant. We are all part of the human race and have a God-given responsibility to care for one another.

Deuteronomy 23:18

*You must not bring the earnings of a...prostitute
into the house of the LORD*

I was under the impression that some things were a given,
but people never cease to surprise me. The fact that God
had to put this command in Scripture doesn't say a whole
lot for mankind, does it? First of all, it says that no man or
woman is to become a shrine prostitute. Now remember,
He wasn't speaking to the world at large, He was speaking
to His people! They had to be reminded that they were not
allowed to become prostitutes.

Secondly, they were told that they were not to use the
money they earned from prostitution for the Tabernacle
or Temple. Hello? Did you hear that? It's actually in the
Bible! It's amazing what they thought was okay to do.
When we come out of the world, we need to come all the
way out. We need to leave our old lives and mentality also.

New believers are especially prone to this. Those of us
who are mature believers need to come alongside and
disciple them in love and in humility. We need to build
the kingdom of God in righteousness.

Deuteronomy 24:21

Do not go over the vines again

In ancient times, during harvest season it was customary to only go through the fields and vineyards once. You only took what you needed; the rest was to stay behind for the poor and for the widow. What a beautiful principle.

Over and over again, God commands us to care for the widow and the orphan. This Scripture is yet again one of many that command us to reach out to the poor among us. Did you know that caring for the poor is not an option? It's required by believers to do so.

Following God isn't like buying a new car. You don't have the luxury to only take the options you want. You don't get to choose eternal life but not buy the "help the poor" package. It's all or nothing. The same goes for the Word of God. This work is focusing on the same Torah that Jesus read.

If the world still worked like that today, we could abolish poverty. Just some food for thought...pun intended!

Deuteronomy 25:9

Take off one of his sandals

Let me start this devotional with a warning…this one is a difficult one for us in modern times to understand. The custom at the time was that if two brothers were living together and one was married, and the married brother died, the unmarried brother was to marry the widow and give her a son to carry on his deceased brother's name. Are you still with me? So far, so good, right? Now, if the brother did not want to marry his brother's wife, she was to go in front of the elders and remove one of the brother's sandals and then spit in his face.

Now it starts to drift into the realm of "differentness." Why the sandal? Because in ancient times when you were prepared to redeem someone, removing your sandal was the signal. Because the brother was unwilling, she was signifying that she would have to do it herself. God told Moses to remove his sandals at the burning bush, right? Why? Because it was holy ground, or was there more to the story? Remember that the removal of sandals was equated with redemption. God was telling Moses that He was going to use him to redeem His people. Wow!

Deuteronomy 25:18

When you were weary and worn out, they met you on your journey and cut off all who were lagging behind

Were you an athlete in school? I played soccer and hockey. The most difficult part of being on the team wasn't the actual game itself; it was the practices that wore you out. The coach would run you up and down the field until you were ready to drop. If you couldn't keep up with the rest of the team, no matter how good you were you got cut, because a team is only as strong as its weakest member. This is what the passage is referring to. As the entire camp was sojourning through the wilderness, some of the people became weary and started lagging behind. This enabled the enemies of Israel to cut them off and trap them.

Many of us become weary in our walk with God sometimes. I know that life can be difficult and unfair sometimes, and it can knock the wind out of you when you least expect it. But we have to remain strong. If we fall behind and start drifting away from the protection of the group, we risk getting cut off and captured. I pray that God will give you strength and cause you to rise up on eagle's wings.

Isaiah 54:10

Yet my unfailing love for you will not be shaken

Israel was always on the cusp of being destroyed or being run out of the country by someone. If it wasn't the Syrians, it was the Babylonians...or the Romans or the Greeks, and on and on the list goes.

In AD 132, the Romans were finally able to totally destroy Jerusalem and the last Jewish revolt. The Jews were exiled again from their land, and this time the exile lasted nearly two thousand years!

God knew the people would be scattered around the earth and that they would feel alone and abandoned. He foretold of a time when no one would accept them, when they would suffer humiliation; that the mountains would shake and move them from place to place. But here, through the prophet Isaiah, he asserts His unfailing and unwavering love for His people.

He extends the same offer to you. If you feel alone and rejected and it seems like no one is there for you, He will be. With His unfailing love He will keep you.

Deuteronomy 26:1

*When you have entered the land the L*ORD *your God is giving you*

This is a very encouraging verse. Notice that it doesn't say *if* you enter the Promised Land, but *when* you enter the Promised Land. What a reassuring thought. No matter where you are on your journey, know that you will get to where He has promised. Some people have been on the journey to their promised land for a long time. In fact, some of you may be on that journey right now. Don't worry about how long it takes you to get there; you will get there at the perfect time for you. Once the people entered into the land, they were to take some of the first-fruits and bring them as an offering to the Lord. Not as a command, but out of a heart of thanksgiving.

Some people know what they want to be from the time they are children. I know people who have told me they always knew what they were meant to be, whether it was a teacher, doctor, or whatever. That never happened with me. I struggled for a long time before I received the call of God on my life. It was a tough journey, but in the end I made it. Here's the encouraging part: you will too.

Deuteronomy 26:19

He has declared that He will set you in praise

Have you ever wanted to be famous? Be honest. I did. As a teenager, I can remember practicing my autograph. I would go through pages and pages until I finally got it to where I wanted. I dreamed of being an astronaut. I was going to be the first man on Mars or discover a new planet or something. Now I'm a preacher... funny how things work out sometimes. I started my journey as a pastor in a small town and I loved it. But slowly God began to move us from place to place, and now to where we are today.

Why do I share this? Because we all have dreams. We all have to believe that we can make it. In today's passage, God told the people that because they had obeyed His commands, He would elevate them and set them as a high praise! Not everyone will rise to the same level necessarily, but we will rise. Everyone—I mean everyone—in the kingdom has an important role to play.

As a body, we all have to do our part. Be faithful to God and let Him be the one to elevate you.

Deuteronomy 27:18

*Cursed is the man who leads the blind astray
on the road*

This part of the Bible isn't always a favorite place to turn to, but nonetheless, it's in the Word of God. I'm talking about the listing of all the curses. Everyone wants the blessings, they love to hear messages about that, but we have to know about the curses as well. How else will we avoid them if we don't even know what they are?

God commanded Moses and the priests to gather the assembly and then read the entire list out loud to the people. And after each curse, the people would recite in unity "amen," or "I agree. I accept the consequences if I break Your Word."

Cursed is anyone who leads a blind person astray. Who would do such a thing? Apparently someone would, so it went in the list of curses. This is one of those verses that has a broader application. Cursed is a person who not only causes the physically blind to go astray, but it also applies to the spiritually blind. Those of us who have seen the light have a responsibility to bring the blind to the light so that they also may see.

Deuteronomy 28:13

*The L*ORD *will make you the head, not the tail*

We're back to the part of the Bible that everyone loves—the blessings for obedience! I have to be honest with you, with all the blessings that God promises for keeping His laws in the Torah, why do so many Christians have a problem with the Torah? I just don't get it. Have you read through all the amazing blessings in Deuteronomy 28?

There is no area of your life that is left out here. He will literally bless every part of your life. Listen to some of the blessings. God said that if you obey His commandments that He will bless your city and your country. Wow! I don't know where in the world you live, but that can apply to you. Had you ever considered that your obedience to God could bring a blessing to your city and even to your entire country? Now that's what I call incentive!

He continues, "I will bless your livestock, your crops, your fields, and your barns." Those all had to do with finances. Are you getting excited yet? And the best blessing of them all: you get the gift of eternal life.

Deuteronomy 28:67

If only it were evening!

Have you ever had one of those days that would just never end? Everything that could go wrong did go wrong? Your computer crashed, you got a flat tire on the way to work, you forgot your wallet on the counter, and so on. You know what I mean—just a brutal day.

All you want to do is get home and put your feet up. All day you keep wishing that it were evening. You just wanted it to end. That's how God says you will feel if you continually disobey Him and break His Law.

Just look back to yesterday and remind yourself of how amazing the blessings for obedience are. Then compare them with the curses for disobedience in this chapter.

Israel was continually going through cycles of obedience, disobedience, and repentance, and then it would start over again. Many of us today go though similar cycles. Let's break that cycle. Let's get serious about God and about His Word. Make every day a day of blessing.

Isaiah 60:1

*Arise, shine, for your light has come, and the
glory of the LORD rises upon you*

The prophet Isaiah had some pretty tough things to say
to and about the nation of Israel. The Lord gave him many
tough words to prophesy to the people. The same prophet
also brought some of the most beautiful words to the Israelites. He speaks with such colorful language and paints a
vivid picture with his words.

One of my favorite memories is waking up to full sun
on the Sea of Galilee. I was in the mountains on the east
side of Galilee—I was actually there writing this book.
Every evening I would watch the sun go down over the
mountains of Tiberias. It is one of the most serene and
beautiful things you will ever see in your life. And then I
came to this verse...Arise, shine!

The power of the earthly sun is one thing, but the
power of the light of God...now that's something entirely
different. Too much exposure to our sun and you can get
skin damage. Too much light from God? There is no such
thing.

Isaiah 60:15

Although you have been forsaken and hated

Have you ever had someone dislike you but you never knew why? I'd like to think that I'm a nice guy and that most people who meet me like me. I remember this one guy in high school who just hated me. Every day he challenged me to a fight at lunchtime. I always walked past him and he never did anything, but still he threatened. Sometimes we are hated without cause.

Unfortunately, no one knows this better than the nation of Israel. To this very day it is surrounded by hundreds of millions of people who hate the Jews and want to drive them into the sea. Yet when you go to Israel, that's not the feeling you get at all. There is a positive and friendly vibe all across the country, from the very north by Lebanon to the extreme south by Egypt. I remember thinking, "How is it possible to be so happy in the midst of such hatred?" I found the answer in this passage. God promised that despite the hatred, he would make them the joy of all generations. No matter who may hate you, remember there is One who will always love you.

Deuteronomy 30:3

*Then the L*ORD *your God will restore your
fortunes and have compassion on you and gather
you again from all the nations where He
scattered you*

We're coming to the end of our time together, and also to the end of Moses' journey with the Israelites to the Promised Land. They haven't even entered into the Promised Land and they are already hearing about a time when they will be scattered all over the earth. What must the people have thought? They were barely out of Egypt. The scars from their taskmasters' lashes had just finished healing, and now they find out that Egypt was only the beginning.

Doesn't life feel like that sometimes? Like it's just drama after drama or tragedy after tragedy. Do you ever feel like telling God enough already? Life is challenging, and at times it can be difficult. But the one constant is that God will be there with you through it all. Don't despair just yet. God told them they would be exiled, but in the same breath He also told them that He would bring them back and that they would be even more blessed. God can and will use all situations to your benefit.

Deuteronomy 30:15

*I set before you today life and prosperity,
death and destruction*

This is a very cool verse. I love the way that God lays the people's choice before them. He actually tells them that what He has given them to do is not that hard. He said that all they needed to accomplish the keeping of His Word was right before their very eyes. He also told them that it was within their reach!

He said that they didn't need to go up to the heavens or across the sea to get the help they needed to observe His laws. What did the people have right in front of them that God may have been pointing to? Each other! All we need are a few good brothers and sisters around us who are like minded. Surround yourself with people from your place of worship and work who have the same values and beliefs. You become like those you hang around with.

Again God is asking us to choose what we want. Do you want destruction? It's there for the taking. But if you want life and prosperity, it's also there for the taking. Let's choose God and His blessings.

Isaiah 61:10

I delight greatly in the LORD

Today this week's prophetic portion starts at verse 10 of Isaiah 61. However, in the biblical period it started at the beginning of the chapter. This weekly portion was the inspiration for this devotional book that you now hold in your hands. The New Testament captures the story for us in the Gospel of Luke, chapter 4.

I talked about this rather quickly in the preface and want to further develop it here. We know that Jesus of Nazareth was a devout Jew, but very few of us understand what that really meant. It meant that He practiced and observed the Torah with all of its requirements. He went to synagogue, celebrated the feasts, ate kosher, and read the Torah every week.

This is the Torah portion that His family had been allotted to read. As the oldest male in his family, the responsibility fell to him to read in the synagogue that week. He didn't randomly select a prophecy that He wanted to fulfill. Before He was born it had been selected for Him. Significant things in our lives don't happen randomly. Pray and ask God for divine appointments, even in the most unlikely of places.

Isaiah 62:1

For Zion's sake I will not keep silent

The nation of Israel had been through the exile and had their Temple destroyed. Once again they had been shamed by their enemies. Anybody and everybody who thought they were something in ancient times picked a fight with Israel and tried to take the land. Reports went out throughout the Middle East about what was happening in Jerusalem, but no one did anything to help. Everyone was busy living their lives and either had no time or interest in helping the Jews.

What a selfish people, you might say. How can anybody stand by and do nothing while mass numbers of innocent Jews are being killed? What kind of cold-hearted people could let such a thing happen? My dear friends, I'm sure the Jews in Nazi death camps were asking themselves the same question. That's why this verse in today's passage rings so true today.

We must stand up for anyone, no matter what their religion or skin color. Like Isaiah says: we must not keep silent.

Isaiah 62:6

I have posted watchmen on your walls,
O Jerusalem

I love God's timing. Only a few days before I sat down to write today's devotional I was in Jerusalem. Not only was I in Jerusalem, but I actually had the chance, along with the other forty-nine members of my tour group, to walk on the walls of the Old City of Jerusalem. I had done it a few times before, but there was something extra special about this time. All I could think about was Isaiah 62:6. It was an amazing experience!

We have been called by God to pray for the peace of Jerusalem. In this day and age, where there is so much anti-Semitism, we as believers need to stand with our Jewish brothers and sisters. As watchmen, it is our responsibility not only to stand with them, but to also keep watch. A watchman watches! We need to watch what the nations are doing and never stop praying for God's peace. Our responsibility may begin with Israel, but it doesn't stop there. We must watch and pray at all times. Pray for your city, and pray for your nation. It's time that we as believers rise to our call as watchmen.

Isaiah 63:7

According to all the LORD has done for us

As you look back on your life, what would you say was the best thing that ever happened to you? Some might say it was the day they got married, or the day they gave birth to their first child. Whatever it was, remember that it was the Lord who gave it to you.

In today's passage the prophet Isaiah is taking a walk down memory lane. He's reminding the people to look back on all that God had done for them throughout the ages. The people were quick to recall the difficult times, but they needed encouragement to remember the good times as well.

What is it about human nature that chooses to focus on the negative or sad moments? Let me explain what I mean. You can have a really nice visit with someone and they could have said a thousand positive and nice things to you, but if they say just one negative thing, that's the memory you walk away with. Am I right? It happens to us all the time. God wants you to focus on the good things that He has done in your life.

Isaiah 63:9

*He lifted them up and carried them
all the days of old*

In today's passage Isaiah is still encouraging the people. He's doing his best to try to cheer them up and to take their focus off the doom and gloom and to remember their better days.

Everyone has had to play the cheerleader at one point or another. Have you ever known people who were happier when they were sad? Does that sound like an odd question? I knew a person who was so depressed all the time, it almost seemed like he didn't know, or didn't want to know, what it was like to be happy. Sometimes we get so caught up in our hurt and sadness that it actually starts to make up part of who we are. Ask anyone who has gone through issues with anger or depression. There's almost a fear of letting go because that emotion has come to define who they are.

That's not how God wants us to live. He wants to remind you of all that He has done for you. How quickly did Israel forget about the ten plagues and the Red Sea? Surely you have had great moments in God. When you're down, focus on those times.

Deuteronomy 31:2

I am no longer able to lead you

All good things must come to an end, so the saying goes. And now, a very good thing must come to an end. I'm talking about Moses. He was pushing one hundred and twenty years of age! His life was split into three even sets of forty. His first forty were spent in Egypt. The second forty he spent as a shepherd. Then at eighty years of age, he began his third and final set of forty.

But after all that he had been through, after all he had seen the Lord do, he knew when his time had finished and when it was time to pass on the torch, in this case, to Joshua. One of the biggest problems that we face in leadership is when the leader doesn't want to recognize that it is time to go. I'm sure that Moses would have loved to be the one to take the Israelites across the Jordan and into the Promised Land. But he knew his time was coming to an end and that it wasn't God's will for his life.

Never get so comfortable where you are that you choose what *you* want over what *God* wants. Know your time; know God's time.

Deuteronomy 31:6

He will never leave you nor forsake you

This is one of the most quoted Scriptures in the entire Bible: "He will never leave you nor forsake you." I'm sure that almost every Christian at some point has quoted it for themselves or to someone they knew. And why not? It's such a beautiful promise. But I wonder how many people are aware of the fact this it comes from the Torah! You see, the Torah isn't as outdated as some people might think.

Moses was getting ready to leave the people. To some of the Israelites, Moses was the only leader they had ever known. Some of them were born after the Exodus and never even saw Pharaoh. Moses was all they knew. When he announced his retirement, I'm sure it sent fear and paranoia throughout the community. They must have wondered how they would make it without him.

That's why this promise meant so much to the people. To be assured that God would never leave them, even if Moses did, was a very comforting thought.

Deuteronomy 31:7

Be strong and courageous, for you must go with this people into the land

Some things are easier said than done. This would qualify as one of those things. Joshua is now the one who has to take the people over into Canaan. Joshua remembers this land well. He was part of the team that was sent to spy out the land. I wonder if he began to think about some of the negative reports the others had made. A land that was filled with giants and large enemies—that's what the others had said. Now he has to step up and go the distance. Moses gives him a pep talk. He looks him straight in the eye and affirms him as leader. He speaks words of encouragement over him. Moses tells him that he must be strong and courageous—not just for himself, but for the people. If the Israelites sensed even for a minute that Joshua was scared, then the whole camp would panic and start to lose heart.

As leaders, we need to lead with the strength and confidence of the Lord. Not arrogantly, but confidently. There is a difference. Arrogance says that you can do it; confidence says that you can do it because God is with you.

Deuteronomy 31:11

You shall read this law before them in their hearing

I think most people would agree that it is spiritually beneficial to cultivate a devotional lifestyle. The question is, how many of us read and study the Bible on a daily basis? Is it something we read a few times a week, or do we just read it at church? Or do we only turn to it when we are in trouble or looking for answers? Moses told the priests that they were to read the Torah to the people out loud, not just once, but several times a year! Wow! I wonder how much more of the Bible we would memorize and understand if we took this advice.

Reading the Bible should be accompanied with studying the Bible. That's why I'm so glad that you are taking the time to do these daily devotionals. Let me encourage you to encourage others to do it as well. I bring a piece of the puzzle to the table, so do you. That's why we all have to do our part together for the kingdom. The Bible is the only book I know of that you can read over and over again and still learn something new every time. No wonder it has been the best-selling book in history!

Deuteronomy 31:16

*They will forsake me and break the covenant
I made with them*

I wonder how God feels when He looks at us. He has
given everything so that we might know Him, and in
return we turn our backs on Him and go after other gods.
God knew we were going to cheat, yet He still betrothed
Himself to us. Could you do that? If you had prior knowledge that the person you were about to marry would cheat
on you after the honeymoon, would you still marry him
or her? It shows me how much God really does love me!

As the people were preparing to enter the land God had
given them, God informs Moses of what he must do next. He
is to take the Law and have it placed in front of the Ark of the
Covenant as a testimony to the people. Each time they went
past the Tabernacle they were to remember the Law. This
keeps in line with what God had said earlier in Deuteronomy, that the people are to write the Law on the door-
frames of their homes as a reminder. Today, this is called a
"mezuzah." I have one on my doorframe so that I will be
reminded of His Law each time I go in and out of my house.
It's a biblical command, not a Jewish thing. Just so you know.

Isaiah 55:1

Come, all you who are thirsty, come to the waters

Have you ever been thirsty? I mean really thirsty? To the point where you got so hot you thought you were going to pass out? When you're that thirsty, there is only one liquid in the world that can quench your thirst: water. Clean, cold water! I remember one trip to Israel with my family. It was in August, the hottest month of the year. The average temperature was 43° Celsius (109° Fahrenheit). No matter which unit of measurement you use, that's hot! I can remember getting out at a gas station in Eilat, and it was windy. I promise you, it was like someone was holding a blow dryer to my face—it was just pure heat. I've never spent so much money on water before, but it was worth every shekel!

Illustrations involving water work really well in the Middle East. It's such a hot part of the world, and anyone from that area would appreciate how refreshing and life giving water can be. In this passage, God reveals Himself as the ultimate thirst quencher—not just physically, but spiritually. If you are thirsty, go to Him. He is the only one who can satisfy your deep, unquenchable thirst.

Isaiah 55:8

For my thoughts are not your thoughts

Who would you say is the smartest person you know? And what makes that person so smart? Did she get good grades in school? Or does he do well in business? I'm willing to guess that some of us think *we* are the smartest people we know! Right? After all, look at all we have accomplished during our short existence on this planet. We've invented the automobile, the television, the Internet, and on and on the accomplishments go. But at the end of the day, we don't even fully understand how the human body, with all of its intricacies and functions.

Yet with our finite minds, we try to figure God out. We want to put Him in a box so we can control Him. If something doesn't go our way, we get all bent out of shape because we saw it happening differently. We need to really understand this passage; we need to let it sink in. His ways are higher than our ways. That means they are better, even if we don't fully understand it at the time. Trust God and know that He has a better plan for you.

Deuteronomy 32:2

Let my teaching fall like rain

The story is getting ready for its crescendo! Moses is right at the very edge of the Promised Land. He's getting ready to hand over the reins to his successor, Joshua, then go up to the mountain to die alone and graveless... and he decides to break out into song! I'm sorry, but I nearly split my sides with laughter as I imagined this playing out in the wilderness! I told you at the beginning of this book that I would infuse my personality into it! But seriously— no, seriously—what a time in his life! This is one of the final times he will address all the people. And he begins by encouraging them to receive the teaching. He calls it his teaching, but it's fully implied and understood that he means the teaching of the Lord. I tell people the same thing everywhere I travel and am given the opportunity to preach. I always tell them to enjoy the teaching, because it's God's teaching. Let it fall like rain, Moses said.

I'm sitting here at a desk in a hotel while on the road preaching, and it's pouring rain outside. Timely! Yes, Lord—let Your words fall like rain.

Deuteronomy 32:18

You forgot the God who gave you birth

These three Torah readings all come from what is known as the song of Moses. It's a look back at his life and his incredible journey. He had seen so much—more than he ever could have imagined possible. From the burning bush to the courts of Pharaoh. From the plagues to the Red Sea. From Mount Sinai to the wilderness, and from there to the Promised Land. All this from a baby who was found floating on a river.

Isn't it like God to use some of the most unlikely characters to accomplish His purposes? I think He does it to remind people that He is the One who is doing it. We are only the vessels that He works through. As the Psalmist says, He is the potter and we are just the clay.

I think that after a while the people started to think that they were the reason why they had made it so far. Don't be like the people in this passage. Never forget the God who gave you life...and who breathed His breath into you when you were still dead in your sins.

Deuteronomy 32:39

I put to death and I bring to life

In this final stanza of Moses' song, he dedicates it to how awesome and wonderful God is. He talks about God having the power to kill and to bring to life. That He has the power to set free and to bring blessing. I agree, He is an awesome God and worthy of praise.

But...can I be honest for a moment? Have you ever experienced a failure, a setback, or an untimely death, and you wondered where God was? People don't like to talk about it, but it's a reality and I think it's important to be open and honest about those feelings. I've had things happen where I didn't understand why God allowed it or why He seemingly didn't do anything about it. We need to talk about these feelings so we can address them, confront them, then heal and move forward.

God isn't intimidated by your questions or by your feelings of disappointment. He is a loving and kind Father. He understands our humanity and our frailty. He gives us the freedom to question. And He waits quietly and patiently for us until we are ready to move forward.

Deuteronomy 32:47

*They are not just idle words for you—they are
your life*

Do words have power? I guess it all depends on how you define power. Can I speak to a waterfall and make it go backward? No. Can I make a universe simply by declaring it? No. Only God has creative power in His words. Can I encourage others to rise up and take the mantle that God has given them? That's pretty powerful. Can I speak in anger and judgment and destroy someone's confidence? That's pretty powerful too.

So I guess the answer is yes, that our words do have power—power to build up and power to tear down. Moses says the same thing to the people. He wants them to understand that the Torah and the Word of God aren't just ancient words scribbled on some piece of paper, but the words themselves are alive and they have the power to give life to those who choose to read and to live them! Wow.

Do you watch your words? Do you speak out of anger and then wish you could take it back? Understand that you have the power of life and death in your tongue: use your words to bring life.

368 "Haazinu"

Deuteronomy 32:52

You will see the land only from a distance

This isn't the first time that Moses is reminded that he will not be the one to lead the people into the Promised Land. It's been said many times before, but I waited until now to deal with it for a reason. I was so impressed with how Moses carried himself despite the impending doom that had been told to him by God Himself. I wanted you to see the character of a godly man who only does what he does because he is doing it for God.

It was Moses and not Joshua who performed all the mighty acts in Egypt. It was Moses and not Joshua who spoke with God on a face-to-face basis. Yet it is Joshua and not Moses who will not only lead the people into the Promised Land but enjoy all the blessing that comes with it.

Moses willingly steps down here and shows us that actions speak so much louder than words. You can go around all day long telling everyone that you're a Christian, but no one wants to *hear* it . . . they want to *see* it. God has called us to live a life of action.

2 Samuel 22:7

From His temple he heard my voice

Today's first prophetic portion was selected by the rabbis for an obvious reason. The Torah portion records the song of Moses, and the prophet portion records the song of David. Two different men who lived at different times, but they both served God with a passion. They both made mistakes, mistakes that they paid for, but nonetheless, they loved God with all their heart.

In verse 7 David talks about crying out to the Lord and hearing His voice from the Temple. It's interesting that God called David a man after His own heart, yet He never spoke to David the way He spoke to Moses, face to face, voice to voice.

I bring up this point to encourage you. Don't worry about what others say their relationship with God is like. Many have claimed to see God and to hear His voice audibly. I wasn't there, so I can't confirm or deny any of it. But God does speak to you all the time. You just have to start recognizing His voice. It's often in the whispers…it's in you.

2 Samuel 22:26

To the faithful you show yourself faithful

I'm thankful for the life of David. For many reasons, but also for the simple reason that it gives me hope. David was a very interesting character. He danced naked, he killed a woman's husband because he got her pregnant, and he was also the king of Israel. Moses was great; so great that sometimes I felt like I could never achieve the level of intimacy with God that he had. But then David comes along and he's like me, he makes mistakes and he loves God fiercely.

David's song, like Moses' song, is a look back on his life and how God was always there for him. David remembers the faithfulness of God over the years, when he was faithful, and even when he wasn't so faithful. I'm so glad that it was God who took it upon Himself to keep the covenant. He knew we could never do it, that's why He shouldered all the responsibility.

Here's something to think about. What would your life-song look like? What kinds of things would it say?

Deuteronomy 33:1

This is the blessing that Moses the man of God pronounced

This is it! The moment has been building and building for Moses. He was living on borrowed time. His days were numbered. This is *the* last and final time he will ever have to speak to the people of Israel. After forty years together in the wilderness, he became so much more than just a leader to them, and they became so much more than just a people to him. He was their father and they were his children, with all the good and bad that comes with such a relationship. He poured his heart and soul into them. He gave up everything so they received the promised blessing of a land of their own so they would be slaves no more.

If you knew you were about to die, what would you say? What would I say? I remember when my dad died. It was the saddest day of my life. But his overall death was beautiful. Even when he could barely speak, he mustered his strength to encourage a family member to get right with God.

We need to use every breath, even our dying breath, to speak life. Remember, our words are powerful.

Deuteronomy 33:12

Let the beloved of the Lord rest secure in him

What brings you peace? What brings you comfort? What makes you feel secure?

Everyone will answer these questions differently. Moses reminds one of the tribes of Israel that the way to find rest is in the Lord. During his farewell speech he addressed all the tribes and had a word for them all. This is the word that he spoke to the tribe of Benjamin. If you will remember, Benjamin was the youngest of Jacob's twelve sons.

People will spend all their money and all their time chasing after things that will make them feel better, that will give them rest. People chase money and pursue material things to the point where they will even destroy their own lives in its pursuit. No matter what you chase or how much you chase it, it will never truly bring you rest or peace.

The only thing that will bring you true rest is knowing that your place in eternity is secured. Place your faith in Him today, and you will have eternal rest.

Deuteronomy 33:16

The favor of Him who dwelt in the burning bush

This final blessing is given to Joseph. Joseph is my personal hero, not just because we share the same name and because the Bible calls him handsome! But seriously, Joseph was a man devoted to God beyond anything I have ever seen. We all complain sometimes because of the "difficult" circumstances we find ourselves in. I suppose that the term "difficult" is relative.

I think we can all agree that Joseph found himself in many difficult situations—ones that we can't even begin to relate to. He was despised by his brothers from youth simply because he had a God-given dream. He was sold into slavery, wrongfully accused of rape, and thrown into prison; he was raised up only to be thrown down again. But through all of it, he kept his relationship with God. Moses said that the tribe of Joseph had the favor of Him who dwelt in the burning bush. What a cool way to refer to God.

I want the favor of God in my life; I also want it for your life. My prayer is that you will walk in God's favor.

Deuteronomy 34:6

To this day no one knows where his grave is

The title in my Bible for this passage is "The Death of Moses." I know that everyone has to die, but what a loss for the people. A great man was lost that day. By himself, Moses climbed up to the top of Mount Nebo. As I write this, I was just there not even a week ago, looking at Mount Nebo from in front of Jericho. I was thinking about this very passage.

From the mountaintop, God showed him the whole area of the Promised Land. What a feeling that must have been for Moses. To think back on everything that had happened over the last forty years, and here it was in front of him. The reality of it must have been overwhelming. Like a painter who spends years on a portrait—what satisfaction to stand back and see the completed task!

Verse 5 says: "And Moses the servant of the LORD died there in Moab." To this day no one knows where his grave is. Even now, Moses deflects all the glory away from himself and unto the Lord.

Joshua 1:2

Moses my servant is dead

Moses' call ended as abruptly at it had started. Moses had just died, and the opening statement in the book of Joshua is a command to get going. There was no time to lose. The man of God is dead, but God is still alive and His plan still needs to be carried out. And just like that, Joshua is in charge and getting ready to cross the Jordan River and usher in a new era for the people. The text doesn't say much about it, but I'm sure Joshua was shaking in his boots! Talk about having big shoes to fill. Have you ever been the replacement for someone who was totally awesome at the job he did, and now you had to step in and measure up?

You see, that's the key. You can't measure up, nor should you. If God wanted another Moses, he would have kept him alive and let him do it. He needed a Moses for stage one, but he needed a Joshua to finish the job. Don't compare yourself to anyone else. God needed *you*! That's why He made you. You're the best *you* in the world! You can be confident in your call, no matter who was before you.

Joshua 1:5

As I was with Moses, so I will be with you

Even though God needed a Joshua to take the people over to the other side, I'm sure that Joshua was relieved to hear that God would be with him as He had been with Moses. What a comforting thought for the new guy!

That must have conjured up all kinds of images in Joshua's brain. He must have thought of how God had parted the waters for Moses. Would He really do that for Joshua? Yes. He did it only a few chapters later. Although Joshua had been appointed by Moses and anointed by God for the task, there still had to be that little bit of doubt floating around somewhere in the back of his mind. It's crazy to think that he would doubt his call after all the affirmation he received from God, Moses, and the people.

I bet you feel the same way sometimes. You know that God has called you, but there is always that lingering doubt. Let me give you the same advice that God gave Joshua: *"Be courageous, be bold. As I was with Moses, so I will be with you."*

Joshua 1:8

*Do not let this Book of the Law depart
from your mouth*

We have now spent 378 days reading and studying the Torah together. I know that for me, the experience has greatly enriched my understanding of the Old Testament and of God. I've been in Christian ministry for a long time, but had never really committed so much time to one specific part of the Bible.

The Lord was admonishing Joshua to meditate on His words. Not only do we start to act like the people we are with, but we will also begin to think and speak like them. Let me encourage you to hang out with Abraham, Isaac, and Jacob. Spend some time with Moses and Joshua as well. How can we do that? By continually reading the Holy Scriptures. God's Word is life to us. It is what guides and directs us. The more time we spend in His Word, the more we will begin to act and think like Him. Let this final verse bring you encouragement.

> *Do not let this Book of the Law depart from your
> mouth; meditate on it day and night, so that you
> may be careful to do everything written in it.
> Then you will be prosperous and successful.*

About the Author

JOE AMARAL is a licensed and ordained minister and travels full time as a sought-after conference and event speaker. Amaral is the host and producer of a weekly television show filmed on location in Israel called *First Century Foundations*. His close work with the archaeological and religious community in Israel affords him a unique perspective and opportunity to gain special insight into first-century life and culture. Amaral has produced several teaching DVDs on the subject of Hebraic roots as well as several documentaries about Israel. Amaral continues to travel to Israel on a regular basis to further his studies in addition to conducting tours. He lives with his wife, Karen, and family in Ontario, Canada.

Notes